Hidden Recipes

A Holocaust Memoir

Hidden Recipes

A Holocaust Memoir

EVA MOREIMI

SecondGen Press, LLC
Minneapolis, MN

Praise for *Hidden Recipes*
A Holocaust Memoir

"Eva Moreimi movingly tells the story of her family, her father Ernest, slave laborer in German Allied Hungary, her mother Ica and Aunt Babi and their journey from a life of comfort into the world of Auschwitz, their survival and liberation and then their journey back from the abyss…Read the book and be moved by the story of courage and determination, loss and dehumanization but also the struggle to resist both physical and spiritual annihilation. Bake from these Hidden Recipes but only if you make two commitments: Serve these cakes on a joyous occasion — these women suffered enough…Above all, tell their story for they must be remembered."

—**Michael Berenbaum, Director of the Sigi Ziering Institute,**
Professor of Jewish Studies, American Jewish University

"From courage to cuisine, this incredible story shows how the best of humanity can survive in the darkest of times. Hidden Recipes captures not only an amazing story of Ica's heroism and survival, but a story of struggle and redemption as scraps of paper will keep alive the memories of joy for generations to come."

—**Steve Isakowitz, Space Industry Executive, Child of**
Holocaust Survivors

"Hidden Recipes is a loving tribute to Elena and Ernest Kalina by their daughter Eva. Elena's recipes are a legacy to her family and an honor to those women who shared their favorite dishes with her in the camp. Because of her act of resistance these women will live on through their recipes."

—**Jodi Elowitz, Director of Education, Nancy & David Wolf Holocaust**
& Humanity Center

"Eva Moreimi's book is a unique Holocaust survival story. In the most unlikely of places, while starving, the women shared with Ica, the author's mother, their most precious family recipes. Ica risked everything to scribble down the recipes, and in an act of defiance and a quest to preserve her culture, she hid them. A fascinating story of uncanny coincidence and serendipity, resilience and defiance."

—Janet Horvath, Cellist, Child of Holocaust Survivors, Author of
Playing (Less) Hurt and her upcoming memoir,
Piercing the Silence

"Hidden Recipes: A Holocaust Memoir is Eva Moreimi's loving ode to her parents, Ica and Ernő, fulfilling her silent promise to herself to honor her parents by keeping the memory of their Holocaust story alive.

Eva tells their story in straightforward style without any of the sappy sentimentality that could all too easily seep into such a narrative. Yet never losing the pathos of her parents' and other family members' tragic tale. When Ernő is conscripted, yet again, into a forced labor brigade, he is allowed to come home to visit his family. As he takes leave of his parents on this one occasion, his father bestows on him the Hebrew Priestly Blessing customarily reserved for smaller children from their father on the Sabbath. When you learn that this is the last time Ernő sees his parents, you feel as if your heart is tearing from your chest.

Despite the loss, deprivation and fear ever present, you feel that hope is right around the corner for our main characters. Ernő's close calls are aided by small kindnesses, unexpectedly from Gentiles. Ica's acts of uncharacteristic resistance in preserving the precious recipes staved off the grinding hunger of starvation for the women of Auschwitz. All these are inspirational and give us hope that tragedy can be overcome.

Finally, Eva gives the reader something important and not usually included in a Holocaust survivor's story…she places a lens onto her own experience of growing up under the shadow of her parents' experiences and, in doing so, gifts us with the missing link of the consequences of the Holocaust."

—Renee Firestone, World-Renown Fashion Designer, Survivor of
Auschwitz, International Holocaust Educator/Lecturer

Library of Congress Control Number: 2019911851

Cover design and book layout by Megan Ellen Johnson.

Cover photo and images:
Ica and Ernő on their honeymoon in 1947.
From Moreimi family archives.

S.C.250 – *Sprengbombe Cylindrisch* was a high-explosive bomb built by Germany for use during World War II (250 kg / 550 lb).

R. Mine 43 anti-tank mine – the German *Riegel* mine was used during World War II (9 kg /20 ½ lb).

The English translation of the Priestly Blessing is reproduced from Renov Edition: Shabbat and Festival Siddur by Rabbi Nosson Scherman and Rabbi Meir Zlotowitz. Used with permission from the copyright holders: ArtScroll/Mesorah Publications, Ltd.

ISBN Number: 978-1-7334097-0-4

Printed in the United States of America.

This book is dedicated to the loving memory of my parents, Elena and Ernest Kalina, whose courage, love and exemplary life are an inspiration to our family.

To the loving memory of my four grandparents and extended family, whose lives were cut short, and to my aunt Babi, my mother's sister, whose existence gave my mother purpose and strength to survive the atrocities.

To the women who so lovingly shared their recipes with my mother and to the six million Jews who perished.

May they be remembered always!

About the Author

Eva Moreimi grew up in Czechoslovakia as an only child to two Holocaust survivor parents. Shortly after graduating from Economic School, she escaped from the communist regime and immigrated to the United States. She lives in the Midwest with her husband close to their three children and six grandchildren. She enjoys reading, practicing yoga, traveling, cooking, baking and spending time with her family and friends.

www.EvaMoreimi.com
HiddenRecipesMemoir@gmail.com

Disclaimer

This book is a memoir. I have done my best to tell a truthful story, and no events have been fabricated. It reflects my parents' recollections of their experiences to the best of their memories. The events are portrayed as they shared with me throughout the years and later during my interviews with them. While all the stories in this book are true, a few of the names have been changed. The recipes were given from memory and I cannot vouch for their accuracy, with the exception of those recipes that were revised and translated into English.

Acknowledgements

My deepest gratitude to everyone who helped make this book become a reality. I am forever grateful to each of you!

I was very fortunate to get advice and support from Joni Sussman, whom I have known for many years. As a publisher, Joni is very knowledgeable. I am grateful for her guidance and vision, and I appreciate her invaluable help.

My heartfelt thanks to Sabina and Andrew Cohen for their assistance with the editing of this book and the many hours they spent helping me. Andrew, a semi-retired Professor of Applied Linguistics, even spent time on the phone with me assisting with lingering editorial issues while he was on vacation with Sabina and their friends in Hawaii. I appreciate their love, support and friendship.

A special thank-you to Rachel Bloom and Nick Pooler. Rachel was very gracious to help me with editing and proofreading. I appreciate her attention to detail and the many hours she spent on this project. Additionally, Rachel's questions prompted me to add more information as well as some clarifications. She was there every step of the way helping me to finalize the manuscript. Her husband, Nick, was a tremendous help researching citations, as well as securing the domain for my website. I am forever grateful to both of them for their kindness.

Nanci Bloom agreed to provide honest feedback from the reader's point of view. I found her critique and feedback very helpful.

My sincere thanks to Meredith Wilson, who so kindly offered editing help. Her suggestions were invaluable, including her help with the overall flow of the story.

Ruth Lauritzen, a friend and former English teacher, also provided editing help and offered a few recommendations. I appreciate her unwavering belief in this project — it means a lot to me.

Thank you to Emily Kleinschmidt and her mother, Kathy Kleinschmidt.

Their feedback and suggestions, as well as their encouragement and belief in my work, are very much appreciated.

I am grateful to Julie Burton for taking the time to read my work. I appreciate her feedback and her belief in the importance of sharing my parents' story.

William Meinecke Jr., who is a historian at the United States Holocaust Memorial Museum, was very helpful in providing a wartime map of Czechoslovakia that shows the southern region annexed by Hungary.

A special thank-you to Danny Gelfman for his assistance with customizing the map of World War II-era Central Europe to show the travels of my parents. He was also very helpful with the old family photographs and photo arrangements of the pastries. I am grateful for his help.

Thank you to Wendy Khabie, who kindly offered to assist with publicity. I am very grateful and appreciate her help.

To all my friends and family who tirelessly listened to me, their love and support mean a lot to me.

To my family, I am forever grateful. To my husband, Jack, for his love and support and for always being there for me. He believed in the importance of my project from the very beginning and often listened to my readings and provided feedback. I can't thank him enough.

To my incredible children, Tommy, Mark and Corinne, who agreed to accompany Jack and me on the trip to Europe, leaving behind their spouses and young children. I am grateful for their help and advice when I needed their input. Their love and support always — and especially while we were in Auschwitz — made this trip possible for me. I could not have done it without them!

And finally, to my great daughters-in-law, Jen and Jody, I am thankful for their kindness and love and for understanding the importance of my children accompanying me on the trip.

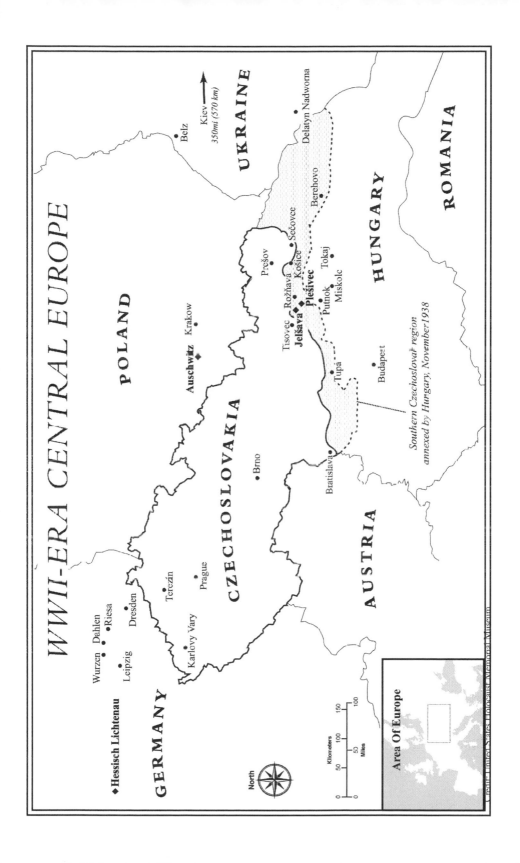

WWII-ERA CENTRAL EUROPE

GERMANY

Hessisch Lichtenau

Wurzen Dahlen
        Riesa
Leipzig   Dresden

Karlovy Vary

Terezín

Prague

POLAND

Auschwitz Krakow

CZECHOSLOVAKIA

Brno

Bratislava

AUSTRIA

UKRAINE

Belz

Kiev
350mi (570 km)

Delatyn Nadworna

Berehovo

Sečovce

Prešov   Košice   Tokaj
      Rožňava Plešivec
Tisovec   Putnok Miskolc
      Jelšava

Tupa

Budapest

HUNGARY

ROMANIA

Southern Czechoslovak region
annexed by Hungary, November 1938

North

Kilometers
0   50   100   150
0   50   100
Miles

Area Of Europe

United States Holocaust Memorial Museum

Table of Contents

1   Introduction

3   Prologue

Part One

9   Ica's Prewar Life

13   Troubled Times for the Kellner Family

15   Shoes by the Danube

17   A Warm Sweater for the Ghetto

20   Meeting Marika

22   A Kiss on the Hand

24   The Angel of Death

28   Vernichtungslager

32   Postcards from Waldsee

35   Music by the Gas Chambers

36   Summoned by the Kommandant

42   Translator and Messenger

44   An Act of Resistance

47   Death March

50   Liberated at Last

53   Journey Home

55   Injustice After the Holocaust

59   Start Life Anew

61   Ica and Ernő Meet

Artifacts

68   Holocaust Artifacts

Part Two

72   Living with Holocaust Survivor Parents

74   Behind the Iron Curtain

76   Immigrating to USA

79   Ica's Sister Babi

80   Receiving a Torah

83   My Parents

85   A Fond Childhood Memory

88   Auschwitz May 2017

91   A Legacy

Part Three

97   The Story of Ernő

103   Kaufmann Family

Photos

108   Family Photos

Recipes

118   Linzer Cookies

120   Ischler Cookies

122   Sour Cherry Cake

124   Gerbeaud Slices

126   Chocolate Almond Torte

128   Wasp Nest (Darázsfészek)

WWII Papers

132   German Forms with Recipes

Endnotes

159   Resources and Endnotes

Introduction

This is a story of my parents, Elena and Ernest. I will refer to them throughout the book as Ica (pronounced Itza) and Ernő, as this is how they were called by family and friends.

My parents are no longer alive, but the story about their Holocaust experiences must be preserved and live on. They overcame many challenges in life and were an inspiration to me. They were my heroes and I looked up to them. I admired them for their courage, for their strong family values and for living life with integrity. Telling their story is my way of honoring them.

Based on a recent survey, there is a lack of basic knowledge about World War II-era genocide. Today there are young Americans who have never heard of the Holocaust, and according a recent study, many American millennials don't know what Auschwitz is. One-third of Americans don't know that six million European Jews were murdered in the Holocaust (also referred to as the *Shoah*) by Nazi Germany and their collaborators.[1] Jews were the primary victims of the Holocaust, but there were many other victims — Soviet citizens, Soviet prisoners of war, non-Jewish Polish civilians, disabled people, the Roma (Gypsies), German political opponents, homosexuals, Jehovah's Witnesses and others.[2]

Today there are very few Holocaust survivors still alive, and it is now the responsibility of the second and third generations to tell their stories. The horrors of the Holocaust were the result of hatred, and we all must learn from it so that history will not repeat itself.

My parents, Ica and Ernő (1996). From Moreimi family archives.

Prologue

Oh, that wonderfully flavorful and rich Hungarian cuisine! Goulash and chicken *paprikás* loved by many. Stuffed cabbage or a cold sour cherry soup and a *rizskoch* eaten on a warm summer day. The delicate, sweet cheese dumplings and delicious plum dumplings rolled in fried breadcrumbs. But nothing tops the fine Austro-Hungarian pastries. These delicate pastries and tortes, yeast cakes, coffee cakes and strudels were enjoyed by everyone, from the Habsburg royalty to the world-renowned composers and writers sitting in famous Budapest cafés discussing their work,[3] as well as others who lived in this part of Europe.

Some of the pastries have been known for a few hundred years, while others were created inside the kitchens of the palace of Emperor Franz Joseph and are still favorites today. Vienna and Budapest remain the world capitals of magnificent and elegant desserts.[4]

These were some of the foods the women in the Auschwitz-Birkenau concentration camp and the Hessisch Lichtenau munitions factory, a subcamp of Buchenwald concentration camp,[5] talked about. Amidst the hunger and starvation, suffering, diseases, bitter cold and death all around them, the women talked about their favorite foods and shared recipes with each other. The memory of prewar life was a powerful survival tool and talking about food was essential because it gave them hope.

These Hungarian Jewish women shared their beloved recipes, which were

3

made with the most delectable ingredients, like chocolate, almonds, hazelnuts, walnuts, figs, chestnuts, rum and butter, as well as fish, poultry, veal and beef. They strived to maintain their humanity, dignity and personal integrity and remained civilized in spite of the Nazis' attempts to dehumanize and degrade them.

After the long shift at the munitions factory ended, they were exhausted, but still had to walk an hour and a half back to the barracks. Upon their return they were required to stand daily at seemingly interminable roll calls to be counted. When they finally got into the barracks, they were not only exhausted, but also famished. They not only talked about food, but often fantasized and dreamed about it. How difficult it must have been to fall asleep on an empty stomach.

I imagine that just before falling asleep was the only time when they could huddle together and talk about food and share recipes. My mother probably wrote not one but a few recipes each night. Did she know how many recipes she collected? I don't think that she ever counted her recipes, as I did only recently. Did the women prepare a complete dinner in their imaginations each night? I will never know the answers to these questions. In retrospect, I wish that I had asked more questions of my mother when she was still alive. I imagine that each night they shared a few recipes. Perhaps one evening it was the Wiener schnitzel with parsley potatoes and cucumber salad. And the next night it was the kohlrabi stuffed with meat or perhaps the liver *pâté* with sautéed onion and garlic with a crusty homemade bread and the well-known Linzer cookies for dessert. Another evening it may have been the recipe of the sour cherry soup and *rizskoch*, a delicate rice cake, with the fine Hungarian scones called *pogácsa* and a *krémes*.

Writing recipes was a form of resistance by my mother. It gave her hope and helped her to maintain her sense of dignity. She suffered so much under the most inhuman conditions, but she remained strong, hopeful and resilient, and she managed to survive. Given the conditions she was under, I wonder how my mother found the time and strength to write so many hundreds of recipes. She had to be very careful to make sure that this indirect resistance was not discovered by the SS guards or the *kapo*. All throughout her life, she had a tremendous inner strength.

Throughout their married life together, it was my mother who was able to tell and retell the story of her Holocaust experiences, their survival and how she always looked out for her younger sister. With pain in her heart and often tears in her eyes, she continued to tell the story. Perhaps it was healing, or perhaps it opened the wounds over again, but she spoke about her experiences, about her parents, about the fellow inmates she was with and about the suffering they endured. She continued telling her story throughout her life, not only to family and friends, but also in schools, synagogues and churches. She believed in the importance of telling the story and to never forget all that she had experienced in the Holocaust in hopes of preventing it from happening again.

My father recounted his wartime experiences in various forced labor camps and his few escapes toward the end of the war, which ultimately saved his life. But to tell the story about his first wife and little daughter and about his parents and the rest of his family was very difficult. It was too painful to talk about them and he always started to cry and was unable to finish. Then my mother would gently step in and quietly finish the story for him.

Now it is my responsibility to continue to tell their story.

PART ONE

Ica's Prewar Life

I lona Kellner, called Ica, was born in 1912 in Pelsőcz, Austria-Hungary, now Plešivec, Slovakia. The Austro-Hungarian Empire collapsed at the end of World War I, and an independent state of Czechoslovakia was founded in 1918.[6]

Life in Czechoslovakia was very good for everyone, including Jews. The first Czechoslovak president, Tomáš Garrigue Masaryk, respected the religious and economic rights of all citizens, and the government protected Jews from antisemitism.

Ica had a beautiful childhood and recalled it fondly. Her father had a successful business in Plešivec, and they had a comfortable life. Her parents, Jolán and Károly (Karl), hired a German governess because they wanted their daughter to learn German, as they spoke German, Hungarian and Czechoslovak.

Ica was lively, spirited and fun to be around. She was well-liked and had many friends. She was a very respectful and well-mannered young woman who had high moral standards. She spent part of each summer vacation visiting family in Tisovec and in Budapest. Her cousins Lenke, a pharmacist and an accomplished violinist, and Lenke's sister Ella looked forward to her visits in Tisovec because she was full of life and brought laughter and fun to their lives. She was confident and cheerful.

Ica took piano lessons; she enjoyed singing and playing the piano. Her parents bought her a beautiful Petrof piano, a well-known brand before the war and used in concert halls across Europe.[7] It was for this reason that her piano was sought out and stolen during the war.

Ica had a very good voice and she liked to sing. Well-known singers and musicians were occasionally invited to Plešivec for entertainment. Ica's friends, without her knowledge, would sometimes tell the guest artists about her voice. Suddenly, she would be called up on the stage and asked to perform a duet. Her performances were met with huge applause and there were often requests for more.

During a sporting event in Plešivec, the organizers of the event hired a pianist and a violinist, both professional musicians who were graduates of a conservatory. Ica was asked to sing at the event. Her mother did not think that it was a good idea for her to sing in public because she had never taken voice lessons, but Ica convinced her to allow it and she accepted the invitation. She chose the famous serenade "Leise flehen meine Lieder" by Franz Schubert. The event turned out to be very successful, and at the end of the performance, people from the audience went up to congratulate Ica. This serenade was originally performed by the famous singer Marta Eggerth, a Hungarian-born American singer and actress.[8]

During one of the summer vacations in Budapest, while Ica was visiting her aunt and cousins, her cousin Vilma decided to introduce her to a well-known singer in Budapest who was a good friend of hers. Ica recalled that the singer was impressed by her voice and told her that it is rare to have such a beautiful voice without training.

Often, when her parents had guests, Ica was asked to play a few pieces on the piano and sing. Her parents, however, would not allow her to have a singing career. After the war her voice was never the same again.

The family had domestic help, but her mother always stressed the importance of Ica learning to cook and bake pastries, yeast cakes and breads. "You never know when this knowledge will come in handy for you," said her wise mother. And so when Ica was home from school, she baked alongside the housekeeper. Ica was a fast learner and impressed everyone with her skills.

After she finished her middle school education, her parents sent her to a prestigious German school in Brno (German: Brünn), which she attended together with her cousin Ella. Brno was a large cosmopolitan city in Czechoslovakia and the center of education, culture and commerce. It was bilingual, with both German and Czech populations.[9] Ica's favorite subjects in school were music, art and German language and literature. She was fluent in Hungarian, German and Czechoslovak.

She fondly recalled that for one of the projects in the art class, she made a life-size African doll. Ica had a petite stature at 5 feet tall and the doll was nearly as tall as she was. She painted the doll's face with large dark eyes and beautiful red lips. She dressed the doll in a nice dress and put a large green hat on her head. When she brought it home, it sat cross-legged in the lounge chair in the hallway. The doll looked very real and anyone coming into the house was startled upon entering.

Ica was an only child until age of fifteen when, in 1927, her sister Vera was born. Family and friends called her Babi. Her parents hired a German governess as they did earlier for Ica. Babi was unruly and would not listen, and the governess quit. Babi did not have the same upbringing as Ica. Life was becoming more difficult for her parents as they were getting older and times in Europe were changing.

After Ica completed school in Brno, she returned home. She became a kindergarten teacher and taught in a Jewish kindergarten in Rožňava, a few kilometers from home. She enjoyed teaching and loved being with small children.

After the war broke out, all of the kindergarteners were deported with their families to Auschwitz-Birkenau concentration camp, where they perished in the gas chambers. These children lived on in Ica's memory and in stories she told of them throughout her life, recalling many of them by their names.

Ica with her baby sister, Babi (ca. 1929). From Moreimi family archives.

Troubled Times for the Kellner Family

C zechoslovakia, the only functioning democratic state in Central Europe after 1933, became Hitler's target for annexations and faced problems with ethnic minorities. The northern and western border regions of Czechoslovakia – Sudetenland, with its Bohemian German population, was ceded to Germany in 1938, another northern region to Poland and a southern region to Hungary. A year later, in March 1939, Slovakia, with the help of Nazi Germany, declared independence. The following day Nazi Germany occupied Czechoslovakia. Czechoslovakia was greatly weakened by the annexations and was powerless to resist the occupation. Bohemia and Moravia became a protectorate of Nazi Germany.[10]

In the 1930s, Nazism in Germany was on the rise, as was antisemitism in Andrej Hlinka's Slovak People's Party in Slovakia. In the early 1940s, the fascist Slovak leadership was so eager to get rid of Jews that they paid the Nazis for every Jew expelled in exchange for a promise that the Jews would never return to Slovakia.[11] Over 80 percent of the Jewish population of Slovakia perished.[12]

The southern part of eastern Czechoslovakia (currently Slovakia), including the town of Plešivec, was forced by Germany to cede to Hungary.[13] A treaty called the First Vienna Award was signed in Vienna's Belvedere Palace in November 1938.[14] Ica and her family, who were Czechoslovak citizens, now were citizens of Hungary. The partition of Czechoslovakia determined the fate of the Jews. Those who lived in the Protectorate of Bohemia and Moravia as well as the Jews of Slovakia were deported in the early 1940s. The Hungarian Jews were the last to be deported.[15]

Life was very stressful and becoming more difficult. Hostility toward Jews and discrimination against them was rapidly rising. Anti-Jewish laws and regulations stripped Jews of their civil rights. Ica's father's gallstones returned, and he was not well. Often in the past he traveled to the famous spa in Karlovy Vary (Carlsbad), which was known for its healing thermal springs.[16] But now he no longer was allowed to even see a doctor. Curfew was established and Jews could not move freely. Many places were prohibited. Domestic help was forbidden and Gentiles (non-Jews) could no longer work for Jews. Banks closed,[17] and the family only had the money they kept at home. Their telephones and radios were confiscated. They had turned over their valuables and most of the jewelry, including a very special ring that Ica wore all the time. Her mother had taken this ring a few years earlier to Poland to be blessed by the Wonder Rabbi of Belz (present-day Ukraine), Rabbi Aharon Rokeach, who was known by both Jews and Gentiles for performing miracles. Although high on the Gestapo target list, he managed to escape and he survived.[18]

This was when the family opened up the *mansard* (attic) in their home and hid some of the inventory from the family business. The business of textiles, shoes, clothing and funeral caskets was located on the ground floor of their two-story house. Later that part of the house was hit in the bombings. The crumbled walls exposed the items hidden behind it and everything was stolen.

The Hungarian government carried out Aryanization through the expropriation of Jewish businesses. A Gentile, referred to as an *arizator*, was assigned by the government to take over the family business. No compensation was provided to the family. The arizator was Irma Csapó from Plešivec. She did not know how to run a business and often had to ask Ica's parents how to do things. The family was no longer permitted to enter their own store.

Shoes by the Danube

I n June 1941, Hungary joined Germany in the war against the Soviet Union. After the German defeat at Stalingrad, Hungary's losses were substantial and the Hungarian government tried to back out of the alliance with Germany. This was not acceptable to Germany and German troops invaded Hungary on March 19, 1944.[19] Adolf Eichmann arrived in Budapest the same month and was in charge of deportations of Hungarian Jews, the largest remaining Jewish population in Central Europe. Even Eichmann was surprised to see how enthusiastically the Hungarians collaborated with him.[20]

Before the war Ica spent many summer vacations in Budapest visiting family. *Numerus clausus* was introduced in 1920 in Hungary to limit the number of Jewish students accepted into the institutions of higher learning.[21] Her cousin, Vilma Mahrer, a few years older, was accepted to the Technical University in Budapest in the early 1920s, at a time when women were not permitted to enroll in the engineering field. Vilma was the first woman to graduate with a mechanical engineering degree in Hungary in 1925. She was well known not only in Budapest but throughout Hungary. Numerous articles were written about her in the newspapers.

Because she was well-known, the Gestapo put Vilma on the top of their most-wanted list during the Nazi occupation of Hungary. The roundup of the Hungarian Jews had not yet begun when the Gestapo drove up to her family's house on Visegrádi *utca* 64 and arrested Vilma. They sent her to Mauthausen, a concentration camp in Austria. She was killed in the camp shortly after her arrival.

The Hungarian authorities together with the *Nyilaskeresztes Párt* (Arrow Cross Party), a fascist organization that controlled the Hungarian government during World War II, were extremely antisemitic and brutal toward Jews. The Arrow Cross Party attacked and killed thousands of people on the streets and the banks of the Danube River in Budapest.[22] Ica's cousin Gábor, Vilma's 16-year-old brother, was attacked and murdered in Budapest.

The Jews who were being murdered on the streets of Budapest were first ordered to remove their shoes, as shoes were an expensive commodity during the war. Then they were shot by the Arrow Cross militiamen into the Danube. Shooting them into the river was convenient because it washed away the bodies. Ica's aunt Fanni, a widow at the time the war broke out, watched from her window as the Gestapo took away her daughter. Devastated after losing both her children, she then committed suicide.

Today a monument called Shoes on the Danube Bank stands near the magnificent Hungarian Parliament Building on the edge of the river to honor the Jews killed on the banks of the Danube during the war. Sixty pairs of period-appropriate shoes were sculpted out of cast iron.[23] The different sizes and styles show that no one — man, woman or child — was spared from the brutality of the Arrow Cross militiamen.

A Warm Sweater for the Ghetto

I ca was 31 years old when the deportation of the Hungarian Jews began in the spring of 1944.[24] Her sister, Babi, was only 16 years old.

There was a faraway look in her eyes each time Ica recalled the bittersweet memory of that day — remembering the last time the family was together in their own house, the beautiful fragrant lilacs in full bloom and her dear mother taking a very last photograph of her in front of the lilac trees.

Hungarian soldiers together with the gendarmerie hired local residents to help move Jews out of their homes. In Plešivec, local residents picked up wealthier Jews and walked them to a place where the Jews were interrogated and beaten with iron rods so that they would reveal where they had hidden their valuables. Ica's family was spared from this torture by the locals.

Ica, her parents and her sister were arrested on May 8, 1944. They were ordered to leave their house and possessions and were forced to move into the ghetto. Given a very short time to leave and under strict supervision, they were instructed to pack only a few items.

Her mother suggested that Ica pack her warm thick sweater, which she had bought for her in Brno. The local Hungarian guard, Mr. Szabó, who was overseeing what was being packed into the suitcase, pointed to the sweater.

"No, you cannot take that one," he said.

"Please, Mr. Szabó, allow my daughter to take this warm sweater. Please," she pleaded.

17

"No, she is not allowed to take that," he insisted.

After the war Ica was on her way somewhere when she saw the guard's daughter, Erzsi Szabó, walking toward her, and to Ica's shock, Erzsi was wearing Ica's warm sweater. The painful memory of her mother pleading with Mr. Szabó flooded back, but Ica passed her without saying a word.

There were also other residents of Plešivec who were eager to help with the deportation of Jews. A local man, Mr. Takács, was among the men escorting the Jews to be tortured. He worked with Mrs. Juhász in the bank where they sorted the confiscated items, including jewelry and other valuables. The Tóth brothers were in charge of all the items confiscated from the Jews. Rumor spread that they stole and then sold many of the items for their own profit.

Many of the Jews were considerate and generous members of the community and often helped those who were less fortunate. The local residents knew all the Jewish families who lived in Plešivec, yet many of the residents turned against the Jews. Ica's father, Károly, was a kind person who always helped others. If a customer needed a few meters of fabric for a dress or any other merchandise from his store and was unable to pay for it right away, he would say, "Take it, and when you have the money, then you can come back and pay for it." Many of these customers never paid. After the war, Ica found her father's little black notebook where he wrote the names of all the customers who had owed him money.

Not long after the war ended an older Christian woman from a nearby village stopped by to see Ica.

"When my mother died, I bought a casket from your father, but had no money to pay for it. I feel that I will die soon, and I cannot die until I repay my debt," she said to Ica. Out of her pocket she pulled a handful of crumpled paper bills. Ica knew that it must have taken this woman a long time to save this money and she did not want to take it.

"Let us say you have given me the money, so please keep it," Ica said. The woman was grateful and kept the money.

For Ica and her family, the deportations began with rounding up Jews. The Jews of Plešivec and the surrounding towns and villages, including Jelšava (Hungarian: Jolsva), were confined to the Plešivec ghetto.[25] A few houses were sectioned off in three different locations to establish a ghetto, which isolated them from the non-Jewish population. Families were housed in crowded and miserable conditions and were guarded. From this point on, they were not allowed to leave the premises of the ghetto.

The Kellner family was placed in the Kóth family's house with a few other families and next door in the Breitbart family's house was the Kaufmann family.

Meeting Marika

A large transport of Jews arrived by train to the Plešivec ghetto from the surrounding towns. Among them was a beautiful three-year-old girl named Marika. She was in the ghetto with her mother, paternal grandparents, aunts and cousins. Marika had blue eyes like her father and blond, curly hair — the curls also inherited from her father.

The living quarters were very crowded since multiple families were sharing the space, and Marika spent most of the time outside playing in the courtyard of the ghetto, where she often sang and recited poems. Some of the songs she sang were about a daddy who was sent away to a forced labor camp.

Sadly, throughout her short lifetime, Marika saw very little of her own father, who rarely was permitted to go home to his wife and daughter. When he received permission to leave, it was only for a day.

Ica noticed this little girl soon after they arrived in the ghetto, as did others. Marika even attracted the attention of the guard, who asked Ica about her after the war. Being a kindergarten teacher who loved children, Ica stopped in the courtyard to talk to Marika and to meet her mother, Irénke Kaufmann. They were Ernő's wife and daughter from Jelšava. At this time no one could have imagined that after the war Ica and Ernő would be formally introduced and she would become his second wife.

Ica and Irénke enjoyed talking together and a friendship developed. They often met in the courtyard of the ghetto, and Irénke introduced Ica to her mother-in-law. Ica had previously heard of Ernő's family from her father and had even met Ernő's father a few times before the war at the train station.

There were a lot of similarities between the two families. Both of the fathers had successful businesses and were colleagues and friends. They were both well respected, honest and trustworthy and were men of integrity. When they planned to travel out of town for business, they phoned each other to make arrangements so that they could take the same train and travel together. Ica often accompanied her father to the train station and recalled that Ernő's father always got off the train to greet them. He was very distinguished looking, handsome and well-built and always wore a sport suit when traveling.

Ica and Ernő had not known each other before the war, but one day in the late 1930s at the Plešivec train station, a young couple got off the train and the man greeted Ica's father. When Ica inquired about the couple after the interaction, her father told her that his name was Ernő Kaufmann, the son of a friend and colleague from Jelšava. Ernő was wearing an elegant suit with an overcoat and a grey fedora hat, and his young wife, Irénke, with an arm wrapped around his, was wearing a fur coat. They were returning to Jelšava from their honeymoon and stopped briefly in Plešivec.

Ica recalled that in the ghetto Ernő's parents did not look well. His father was thinner, and both of his parents were sad and did not say much. How painful it must have been for them to be confined in a ghetto, not knowing what would happen to them and their loved ones. They also had the responsibility of taking care of two grandchildren while their daughter Klári and her husband were in hiding.

Ica chose to remain single for a while, in spite of her parents urging her to marry prior to the war. Perhaps this was the first stroke of luck that saved her life, although there were many. Young mothers with small children did not survive. After the Plešivec ghetto was vacated and everyone was put into cattle trains, Ica never saw Ernő's wife and daughter again.

A Kiss on the Hand

The Plešivec ghetto was vacated after about five weeks. Everyone was put on trains and transported to a brick factory in Diósgyőr near Miskolc, Hungary. They remained at the brick factory overnight until all the Jews from Miskolc and the surrounding counties were gathered. They were under the watchful eyes of armed guards and had no idea where they were being taken or what was awaiting them.

They spent the night in the rain lying on the wet ground of the brick factory. When Ica awoke abruptly in the middle of the night, she found that rather than sleeping, her mother was keeping vigilant during the night. In fact, her mother was kissing her hand.

"Mommy, what are you doing?" Ica asked.

The custom during those times was for the child to kiss their parents' hand and not the other way around, as a gesture of respect and courtesy. Her mother stayed awake that night covering her two daughters as best she could and watching over them. She wanted to take off her coat to cover them, but Ica did not allow her to take it off. She told her daughters what good children they were and how much she loved them.

The Nazis took over the transport from the Hungarian authorities at this location on June 13, 1944. They herded everyone into cattle trains. The Nazis intentionally misled them by telling them that they were being temporarily relocated for work. They had no idea that the Nazis had a very carefully orchestrated plan of genocide.

The cattle trains were very crowded and people were tightly packed together. It was such a traumatic experience that Ica could not recall many of the details — except that the journey took three or four days and that they were not given food or water at all during this period.

Occasionally the train would come to a stop, then after a while it resumed the journey. It often waited for more important military trains to pass. There were no windows, only a very small opening with bars on one side. The doors remained locked at all times. A bucket was provided for bathroom use. She remembered standing, unable to move or sit down due to lack of space, and unable to sleep. Since it was summer, it was very hot and stuffy inside the windowless wagon; there was not enough air to breathe. She recounted that the conditions were so miserable that the people were beside themselves and in no state to talk much with each other. People were dehydrated and exhausted from hunger. By the time they arrived at their destination, there were many dead among them.

The Angel of Death

Finally, the cattle train came to a stop and the doors were thrown open. The daylight was blinding after being locked in darkness for days. Then they were forcefully herded out of the train onto a nearby platform.

Ica never forgot her first impression when she stepped off the train. It was an eerie feeling seeing a vast area — no grass, no trees, heavy smoke coming out of the chimneys and a terrible stench in the air.

It did not take long to find out the horrific truth that it was the smell of burning flesh. They had arrived at Auschwitz, also known as Auschwitz II or Birkenau, the largest of the Nazi concentration and death camps in Poland. They had never heard of Auschwitz before. For many, the Birkenau killing center was their final destination, the last stop. It was the middle of June 1944.

On the platform there was chaos, with men in Nazi uniforms screaming out orders, accompanied by vicious dogs that were barking at them and ready to attack.

"*Raus! Schnell!*" ('Out! Fast!')

Among the *Schutzstaffel*, the SS troopers, were male prisoners in striped garments helping to remove people from the cattle trains as rapidly as possible. They were ordered to leave their luggage behind. They never saw it again.

The process of selections began. Josef Mengele, the chief physician of Auschwitz, who was nicknamed the Angel of Death, decided with a wave of his hand who would live and who would die. In a split second he determined who would be kept for temporary work and who would be sent directly to their death. Impeccably dressed in a black SS uniform, he would greet every incoming train to Auschwitz-Birkenau. Around 90 percent of the new arrivals were immediately sent to die, among them the elderly, mothers with children and pregnant women.[26] Mengele also became known for his inhumane medical experimentations on Auschwitz prisoners. He was particularly interested in experimenting on twins and dwarfs. He operated on them in inhuman ways and tortured to death many children as well as adults.[27]

Men had to form separate lines from women, and Ica's father, Károly, was immediately separated from his family. Everything was done in such a rush that he never had a chance to say goodbye to his loved ones. He looked back at them with sad eyes and waved as he was hurried away with the rest of the men. This was the last time his family saw him.

The Jewish prisoners in the striped garments were strictly forbidden to speak to the deportees. In spite of this, whenever they had an opportunity, they tried to help — especially the weak and the elderly — while they were directing the crowd.

The women found out from these prisoners that the mothers with young children and the older people were being separated from the rest. They suggested to them that, if asked, they should claim to be above the age of 16 and under the age of 40. In this age range they would have a better chance of being selected for work. Ica and Babi decided not to reveal their real ages. Instead, Ica subtracted a few years and Babi added a few years.

The women were instructed to form a line and were rushed to move forward. When they got in front of Mengele, he pointed to Ica's mother, Jolán, and sent her to the left while her two daughters were sent to the right.

Ica quickly took hold of her mother's arm and addressed Mengele in German.

"Please allow my sister and me to stay with our mother," she said.
Mengele looked at her, grabbed her by the arm and without a word pushed her back to the right side. Then he sent her sister to the right also.

They did not have time to say goodbye to their mother. Ica looked back and saw that her mother started to cry. A family friend, Mrs. Margit Löbl, put an arm around their mother and was comforting her as they were being taken away in a hurry. Ica and Babi never saw their mother again.

A Polish Jew wearing a striped garment went up to Ica and gestured toward Mengele.

"Do you know who this man is? This is Dr. Mengele. He touched you. Usually he never touches Jews," he said to her.

The herding of people out of the freight cars and onto the train platform took place very rapidly, despite the seemingly chaotic way it was done. During the entire selection process, the Nazis were very careful to try to avoid violence toward the Jews because it was important to them to execute everything efficiently and smoothly without any resistance from the Jews.[28]

After both of their parents were taken away, Ica turned to a Polish Jew in a striped garment.

"Please tell us where they took our parents," she asked.
The prisoner pointed to the thick smoke coming out of the chimneys and said,

"Do you see that smoke up there? That is where your parents are!"
This is how they found out that their parents were murdered. It did not take long to hear about the existence of gas chambers and the crematoria where the bodies were burned in ovens.

Ica and Babi, with the rest of the women who were at least temporarily deemed fit for work, were taken to a bath house, the so-called sauna. They were ordered to undress and leave all their clothes in one big pile. With the help of scissors and razors the prisoners in charge of this work hurriedly shaved off the hair on the women's heads and on the rest of their bodies. After a very brief shower, while still naked and wet, they were pushed into another room and sprayed with a disinfectant. They felt humiliated when they had to strip naked in front of everyone and were shaved by male prisoners. They were told that their hair was shaved off in an attempt to control lice, which spreads typhus, but in reality the hair was used to manufacture industrial felt and was also made into a yarn among other uses.

While still naked, they were pushed outside and instructed to quickly grab one piece of used clothing from a large pile. Some women got clothes that were too small, others too big. All of the clothing was worn-out and ragged. Later in the barracks, they swapped items with one another.

Ica got a light summer coat made from a very thin fabric. She also got a pair of wooden clogs with a tie on top. Not everyone was lucky enough to get shoes; some women were barefoot. Ica wore this one piece of ragged clothing the entire time, both in summer and winter. They had no underwear. Babi also got a light summer coat, but all the buttons were missing. A large red cross was painted on the back of their clothes.

Their own clothes were confiscated and sorted out into separate piles by the *Kanada Kommando*, deportees assigned to this work.[29] To the deportees, Canada was a country that symbolized wealth; therefore, they named the warehouse facility *Kanada*.[30] The enormous mountains of clothing, shoes, suitcases, eyeglasses, flatware, combs and brushes were collected in the *Kanada* warehouse facilities and transported to Germany for the use of the German civilian population. The hair shorn from the heads of prisoners selected for labor, and the corpses (after the bodies were removed from the gas chambers and before being incinerated) were piled into heaps and sold to German companies for use in many products.[31] Watches, wallets, shaving kits and food, especially delicacies, were given to the SS soldiers. Jewelry, cash and the gold teeth ripped from the mouths of the dead and melted into gold bars were shipped to the *Reichsbank*, the German central bank. By stealing just a few grams of jewelry from individual Jews, the SS came to possess several tons of precious metals. The deportees strengthened the German military and helped finance their own destruction.

The deportees who were not sent to the gas chambers right away were registered as prisoners. Their registration numbers were tattooed on their left arms. Ica and Babi were among the thousands of Hungarian women who were not registered in Auschwitz; the Nazis did not have time to tattoo them.[32] The registration system collapsed with overload when the Hungarian Jews arrived.[33]

Vernichtungslager

Ica and Babi spent seven weeks in Auschwitz-Birkenau, always staying together. In their barrack there were no wooden beds, as there were in the other barracks. Rather, they slept on the floor, tightly packed next to each other.

The deportees were closely watched by the Nazis and were treated brutally and subjected to starvation. The concentration camp was surrounded by high electric barbed wire fences and a few watchtowers with armed SS guards supervising the camp.[34] Prisoners had no chance to escape and those who could no longer tolerate the suffering intentionally ran to the fence and were electrocuted.

Every day they were assembled in rows of ten and were ordered to stand motionless at *Zähl Appell* (roll call). They stood in the early hours of predawn, shivering from the cold, then in the middle of the day under the hot sun with their shaved heads, and then again late in the evening. If they talked or moved, they were shot immediately. The women were hungry, cold and tired. In the early morning hours, they would stand close to each other, some supporting others if they dozed off. Those who fainted or collapsed from exhaustion, hunger or sun stroke were taken away and were never seen again.

Kapos (block prisoners) were assigned by the SS guards to supervise forced labor or carry out administrative tasks in each block (barrack). During the daily roll calls, *kapos* counted the prisoners and reported the number to the SS officer. If it was off by even one number, the counting had to start from the beginning.

Thousands of women stood for hours to be counted over and over again. These roll calls lasting for hours served not only to count the prisoners but were also a form of torturous punishment to weaken, humiliate and intimidate them.

Ica and Babi did not get work assigned to them in Auschwitz-Birkenau. They were among the reserve labor force for the SS. They lingered on for weeks without work and most of their day was taken up by the exhausting roll calls. Due to poor conditions and starvation, many of the women were emaciated and succumbed to diseases. These women were removed during the selections and never seen again. Many died within a few weeks of their arrival as a result of mistreatment, disease and lack of food.

Auschwitz-Birkenau was a *Vernichtungslager*, an extermination camp. By spring 1943 four huge crematoria were fully operational. The four crematoria housed eight gas chambers and forty-six ovens that could dispose of some 4,400 corpses per day. Most of the victims were Jewish, but there were also non-Jewish victims.

During the deportation of Hungarian Jews in spring 1944, thousands of people were selected daily and sent to the gas chambers. The rate of extermination was at its highest point and the SS gassed as many as 6,000 Hungarian Jews each day in Auschwitz-Birkenau.

The gas chambers were built to look like shower rooms to confuse the victims. The majority of new arrivals selected to die were told to take a shower before work. Once they were inside, the massive doors to the shower-like chambers were locked behind them and they were immediately gassed with the highly poisonous gas, Zyklon B. The bodies were cremated in one of the four crematoria that were in operation day and night. The chimneys of the crematoria were smoking all the time and the horrible stench was suffocating.[35]

The wooden barracks were overcrowded and had to be emptied daily to make room for the arrival of the new transports. Selections were conducted daily. Ica witnessed women selected from her barrack and taken to the gas chambers. One day among the group of selected women were the Kohn sisters, who were from Ica's hometown of Plešivec. None of the women knew when it would be their turn to be selected and taken to their death.

Although thousands of people were sent to the gas chambers every day, the aim of the Nazis was to speed up the mass killings.[36] In addition to sending victims to the gas chambers, many people were lined up naked at the edge of multiple large deep pits and shot. At times, the piled-up bodies were set on fire. The smell of burning flesh was everywhere, and was unbearable. At other times the bodies inside the pits were covered with dirt.[37]

Occasionally the male prisoners in striped uniforms pointed out to the women that there were mounds of dirt still moving. Sometimes the bullets caused injuries and the injured were buried alive. They suffered slow, agonizing deaths. Children often survived longer than adults. Ica saw the dirt moving with her own eyes. She also saw a man on the gallows who writhed in pain as he slowly suffocated to death. These memories were very painful and unforgettable.

Food was scarce and inmates were starving. Hunger was a big problem and many died of starvation. The rations were intentionally so small that the food barely kept the people alive. In the morning they were given *Ersatzkaffee*, so-called coffee, which was actually dark brown lukewarm water. At noon they got terrible tasting watery soup. If they were lucky, they would find a potato peel or a piece of turnip inside it. More often they found weeds or grass in the soup. In the evening each person received a small piece of dark bread the size of their palm. The bread tasted more like saw dust than bread. The food they received was so bad that it was difficult to swallow.

Ica did not want to eat all the bread at once and every day she divided it into three portions, saving some for later. People around them were dying of hunger. In spite of the circumstances Ica retained her strong will. She was capable of saving a piece of bread for later, although her stomach was aching for food. She wanted to make sure that she or her sister would have something to eat later if needed. Although she was robbed of everything, she still had the freedom to make her own choices under these horrific circumstances.

Her parents were no longer alive and she felt a strong sense of responsibility toward her young sister and was very protective of her. Now it was only the two of them. Her love and commitment to her sister gave Ica an unwavering will to live.

The summer of 1944 was a hot one in Auschwitz-Birkenau. There were no trees in the near vicinity,[38] and therefore, there was no shade. The women were hot and very thirsty. Sometimes during the roll call a truck passed by with water dripping out the back. Ica saw women running after the truck to catch a few drops of water. They were shot before her eyes. Death was everywhere around them.

One of the SS guards in Auschwitz-Birkenau had contracted tuberculosis while fighting on the front lines. Because he was too sick to fight, he was recalled from the front and assigned to be a guard in the concentration camp. He was visibly ill and could not finish his meals. He ate very little and threw away most of his food. Some of the women ran to grab a piece of food and were immediately shot by the SS. There were others who managed to grab an extra piece without being caught. Ica did not want to be exposed to tuberculosis and asked her sister to stay away from that food. They had to manage on the small portions they received.

The women who had a family member or a friend working in the kitchen were considered lucky. These women sneaked out extra food and shared it with their family and friends. Ica was not one of them, although one day Bözsi, an acquaintance from Jelšava, who worked in the kitchen slicing bread, approached Ica and asked her:

"Ica, did you receive a small piece of bread I sent to you with Vali? You never ask me for food." Ica became emotional and started to cry.

She said, "Yes, thank you, I received the bread you sent with Vali. I don't ask you for food because I know that you have enough people to share any extra food with."

Bözsi was together with her sister Edith in the concentration camp, and after the war they became distant relatives with Ica through marriage. This was the only time that Ica received an extra portion of food.

Postcards from Waldsee

S hortly after the women arrived in Auschwitz-Birkenau, the Nazis distributed postcards and instructed them to write home to their loved ones. They were told to inform their family that they were happy and doing well, had plenty of food and had warm accommodations. The Nazis' intention was to deceive the Jews who were not yet deported into believing that the sender was doing well and is in a picturesque location in order to avoid any resistance. They had to strictly follow the instructions given by the Germans and were prohibited from writing about the true camp conditions.[39] The postcards were censored, and if the rules were breached, it would have resulted in severe punishment, most likely death.

This was one deception among the many deceptions by the Nazis. Ica already knew that their parents were no longer alive; she had learned about their murder on the day of their arrival at the concentration camp from the Polish Jew who pointed to the smoke coming from the chimneys. Even with that knowledge, Ica had no choice but to follow orders, and she addressed the postcard to her mother.

They were instructed to put "Waldsee" for the return address. Waldsee, meaning Forest Lake, was a fictitious name for Auschwitz.[40] Today, a few of these postcards can be found in the Jewish Museum in Budapest, Hungary.

With Ica was her good friend Rózsi Breitbart, who was also given a postcard and instructed to write to her family. After receiving the postcard, her brother tried to find them, but could not locate Waldsee on the map. This was

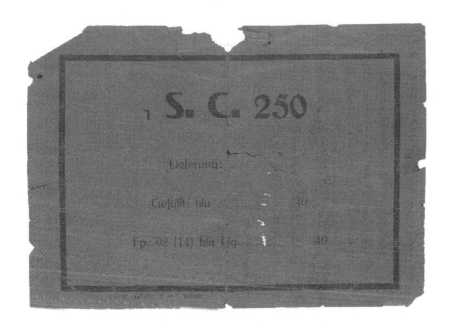

S. C. 250

Lieferung:

Gefüllt: blu   40

Fp. 02 (11) blu 1/9   40

another Nazi deception: instructing people to write Waldsee on the return address instead of the Polish name of nearby town Oświęcim (German: Auschwitz).

Throughout her entire life, Ica always wrote a draft first before writing a letter. This was impossible to do in Auschwitz-Birkenau because they had no access to pen and paper, aside from this one instance of them writing the postcard. A few months later when she was in possession of paper and pencil, she remembered the postcard and wrote down two very similar versions from her memory. She wanted to remember what she had written, and she also wanted it for safekeeping. She kept it among the recipes.

Translation of Letter:

My Dear Mother!

We are happy that we can finally provide you with a sign of life. Remain calm, dearest Mother, we are doing well and are healthy. Please do not worry about us. From the very first moment we are together with Baby. We work and sleep together. We are not cold. We are in warm rooms. We are also writing to our dear Father. Hopefully he will receive our few lines and we will get a reply. We think about our dear parents often and we believe that you are healthy. Dear Mother, look after yourself. Do not forget that we live for one another. If possible, please write us right away, we urgently await your reply. There are many people from Pelsőcz (Plešivec) here. Rózsi, Fischer Magda and Éva, Morvai, the Pinkász sisters, Kató Kellner, Margit and Klári Löbl, Ella Löwy and Vera from Ózd.

We love you very much. Kisses from your loving daughters,
Ica and Baby*

---

* Note: Babi is intentionally spelled with an "i" throughout this book.

Music by the Gas Chambers

The day arrived when Ica and Babi were among the women who were selected to go to the gas chambers. They knew where they were being taken and that death was awaiting them. They did not cry, they just wanted it to be over. By this time they had suffered so much that death was going to be a relief from their misery.

Ica remembered that the orchestra played music near the gas chambers. Music often accompanied selections and mass murder. The musicians consisted of Jewish prisoners who were talented musicians, some of them well-known. While the women stood by the gas chambers awaiting their death, among them Magda Karsai from Plešivec recognized Ica and came up to talk to her. Ica did not recognize Magda right away because her face and head were swollen from the hot sun. Also, everyone looked different without hair.

Ica and Babi, with the rest of the women selected to die that day, stood in front of the gas chambers the remainder of the day and throughout the night. On that day, the Nazis ran out of Zyklon B,[41] the highly poisonous cyanide-based pesticide used for the mass killings. So, they were temporarily saved from being gassed.

Summoned by the Kommandant

O n the morning of August 2, 1944, an order was received from Germany requesting Jewish slave workers.[42] One thousand Hungarian women, among them Ica and Babi, who had been standing in front of the gas chambers through the night, were put on freight trains. They were transported to Germany near Kassel in the Hesse region.[43]

The journey on the train took about two days. They did not get food or water. The women were taken to an underground munitions factory in Hessisch Lichtenau, a subcamp of the Buchenwald concentration camp. The company was called *Fabrik Hessisch-Lichtenau der GmbH zur Verwertung chemische Erzeugnisse*, a subsidiary of Dynamit Nobel. Hessisch Lichtenau munitions factory was one of the three largest manufacturers of explosives in Germany. Located in a dense forested area, the factory was well camouflaged with shrubs and trees planted around it and on the roof and was under strict security by the SS and the Gestapo.

When these emaciated women arrived in the small town of Hessisch Lichtenau, a suburb of Hirschhagen, near Fürstenhagen, the commandant of the camp was shocked to see the condition they were in and told to the SS guards:

"I asked for workers. You brought me skeletons."

He did not want to accept them, but Germany had a labor shortage and he ultimately agreed to take them.

The SS guards took them to the edge of the town, a long walking distance away from the factory. On the camp premises they saw many wooden barracks, called blocks. Most of the barracks were living quarters for the foreign workers, others were administration buildings. The Hungarian women were crammed into one block, a wooden barrack called Camp Clubhouse, which was surrounded by an electrified barbed wire fence. The barrack was cold and damp, with rows of wooden planks for beds, though not enough for everyone.

The women were registered on September 19, 1944, and a small piece of rag with hand-stamped numbers on it was stitched to the front of their clothes. Ica became prisoner number 20409 and her sister Babi 20407.[44]

The work was physically demanding for these malnourished women, filling grenades, mines and bombs with toxic materials that were very dangerous to inhale. Some of the women developed liver poisoning from being exposed to the toxic powders and their skin turned yellow.[45]

Ica had met Magda Horovitz from Jelšava in the Plesivec ghetto. Magda made sure she bent over her workbench closely to do her work precisely, according to the

Concentration Camp Buchenwald, Prisoner Registration Form, Ilona KELLNER, 1.1.5.4 / 7611060, ITS Digital Archive, Arolsen Archives.

instructions. Magda died in the munitions factory from inhalation of the poisonous fumes.

Eva Fischer and her sister Magda Fischer (later Berko) were together with Ica and Babi. They were from Plešivec and were friends of Ica and Babi. Eva developed a sore throat soon upon their arrival at the munitions factory. The toxic materials made it impossible for her to breathe and she died of suffocation. The Nazis were known to keep excellent records, and everything was recorded accurately. The names of both Magda Horovitz and Eva Fischer are listed in the table below.

Dieter Vaupel, a German historian, wrote about the transport of the 1,000 Hungarian women from Auschwitz-Birkenau to Hessisch Lichtenau in his book entitled *Das Aussenkommando Hessisch Lichtenau des Konzentrationslagers Buchenwald, 1944/45: eine Dokumentation. Kassel: Gesamthochschulbibliothek.*

Table 1.
Arrivals and Departures in Hessisch Lichtenau

Date	Arrival	Departure	To/From	Date List Ready	Number of Prisoners
2/8/44	1,000	–	Auschwitz	9/20/44	1,000
8/4/44	–	1	+Eva Fischer		999
8/11/44	–	1	+Anna Kasztl		998
8/31/44	3	–	Auschwitz	10/10/44	1,001
9/24/44	–	1	+Edith Lederer		1,000
10/5/44	–	1	+Magda Horovitz		999
10/8/44	–	1	+Magda Mandel		998
10/27/44	–	206	Auschwitz	10/31/44	792
1/4/45	–	2	Bergen–Belsen	2/8/45	790

Source: Dieter Vaupel, *Das Aussenkommando Hess. Lichtenau des Konzentrationslager Buchenwald, 1944/45.* Kassel: Gesamthochschulbibliothek, 1984, p. 74.

The table above, originally from the book by Vaupel (1984), was reprinted in Studies on the Holocaust in Hungary, which was edited by Randolph L. Braham, translated by Maida Pollock and published by Social Science Monographs (Boulder, CO) and the Csengeri Institute for Holocaust Studies at City University of New York (distributed by Columbia University Press, 1990).[46]

This is the transport that Ica and Babi were in. The two women Ica knew personally who died of inhalation of the toxic fumes are listed in the table. After the women died, the number of prisoners in the last column changed.

The women worked long shifts under strict supervision seven days a week. They were treated as criminals and were forbidden to talk to one another while they were engaged in forced labor. They were expected to work rapidly and with precision. The German foremen were very cruel, and if the prisoners' work did not meet their standards, they simply shot them.

Early every morning they stood for *Zähl Appell* in front of their barrack. Afterward, they were taken by the SS guards on a 1½-hour march from the barrack to the underground munitions factory. In the evenings when the shift was over, they marched back another 1½ hours from the factory to the barrack. They were instructed by their fellow prisoners (among whom were a doctor and nurses) to sing so that they would expel some of the toxic material from their lungs. Ica, who had a beautiful voice and enjoyed singing before the war, did not want to sing. Knowing that her parents were murdered made it impossible for her, and she sometimes cried while the others sang.

After the march back to the barrack, they once again had to stand for *Zähl Appell* and were counted before being allowed to return to the crowded barrack. They were constantly harassed by the SS guards on the way to and from their work at the munitions factory. The SS women used their whips, which they carried at all times. Many of the guards were sadistic and enjoyed torturing the women.

Out of this transport of 1,000 Hungarian women, as indicated in the table to the left, 206 were sent back to Auschwitz at the end of October, because they were ill or could not keep up with the demanding work. Their families were sent along with them. None of these women survived — it is presumed that they were sent directly to the gas chambers of Auschwitz-Birkenau.

Among the women sent back to Auschwitz was Panni. Panni's sister was sick and therefore the healthy young Panni was also selected to go back to Auschwitz. Panni is one of the women who shared recipes with Ica.

Babi and her cousin Vera Weinberger (later Foltýn) worked next to each other. Babi's assignment was to lift the heavy explosives from the workbench onto a wagon.

These explosives were filled with powder and sometimes weighed 50–60 kilograms, well over 100 pounds. She also had to unload the wagon and put the explosives up on a table. This job was very difficult for her given her young age and petite stature. On the daily marches back to the barracks, she would plead with Ica:

"Leave me alone already."

"I can't bear this anymore."

"Let me die."

After losing her dear parents, Ica had only her sister. She was fortunate to stay with her sister throughout their captivity. There was someone she loved and who loved her, someone beside herself to live for and for whom it was necessary to remain strong. She felt responsible for her sister and she always encouraged her sister not to give up.

The SS guards and *kapos* treated them with extreme brutality and anything minor would provoke the most vicious beatings. One day Ica overheard a conversation between two *kapos*, who were discussing that they needed help in the kitchen to peel potatoes. Immediately she thought of her sister, and she politely approached the women with her request. The *kapos* asked her why she wanted her sister to get this job and she explained that the factory work was very difficult for Babi.

That day when the long shift in the factory ended and they were lined up ready to march back to the barracks, all of a sudden four SS women, who were often even more brutal than the SS men, started to hit Ica. They beat her, mostly hitting her head. Ica kept asking them *"Warum?"* ('Why?'), but they would not tell her why. Only later she found out that she was beaten because she had asked the two *kapos* if they could assign the kitchen duty to her sister. The *kapos* complained about her to the SS guards.

Both sisters were in tears. Babi was very upset and said to her sister, "You are suffering even more because of me. Why did you interfere? At the end I did not get the job anyway and they hurt you."

Ica saw how terribly swollen her sister's legs were and how difficult it was for her to work with the heavy ammunition in the factory. It was painful to see her little sister suffer so much. Walking a few kilometers every day from the barracks to the factory and back in the evenings was difficult for all these weak and malnourished women.

In the evening they returned from the factory back to the camp. They were ordered to stand for *Zähl Appell* and were counted. Unbeknownst to Ica, the SS women guards complained about her to the camp commandant. Before the women were allowed to enter the barrack, the commandant stepped out of his office, unlocked the electric wire gate and pointed to Ica.

"*Du kleine komm in mein büro*" ('You, little one, come to my office'), ordering her to follow him.

Ica looked back at her sister and cousins — it was a silent farewell. She followed the commandant until she disappeared behind the electric wire gate and into the building.

They heard rumors that anyone who is summoned to the commandant's office does not come out alive. The commandant and Ica entered his office. She was standing and he leaned with his back against the desk. He began to question her while fingering his pistol.

"Do you know what you deserve?" he asked.

"Yes, I know *Herr Kommandant*, and you will do me a favor if you shoot me, because I cannot take this life any longer," Ica replied calmly. He looked at her surprised.

"Whose daughter are you that you speak such beautiful German?" he asked her.

"My father is a business owner," she responded.

He thought for a moment, then said, "Come."

Ica, determined to remain brave, followed him silently, not knowing if she would be taken to the electric wire fence and shot.

To her surprise the commandant opened the electric wire gate and told her to return to the barrack. When she entered the barrack, she saw her sister, cousins and friends huddled together and crying. They were all shocked to see her alive.

Over the years, whenever Ica thought of this incident, she wondered why the commandant had let her live. Was it because he did *not* want to do a favor to her and spare her more suffering, or was it because he was impressed by her knowledge of German? Perhaps it was both, but she never knew the answer.

Translator and Messenger

Because Ica was fluent in German and spoke *Hochdeutsch*, High German dialect, the Nazis in Hessisch Lichtenau selected her to be their translator. She was also required to carry messages throughout multiple buildings. For this reason, Ica was given a *Fabrik Hessisch Lichtenau* identification pin.[47]

When she did not translate or carry messages, her duties were to clean up inside the factory. These responsibilities allowed her to move around more freely.

One day a man walked cautiously among them asking questions. He wanted to know who they were, where they were from and what they were doing there. The women were frightened by his inquiries and too scared to answer. They knew that if they got caught talking to him, they would be immediately shot by the SS.

Later in the day Ica was summoned. "We need you to translate. Follow me," she was told. The Nazis needed a Hungarian and German translator. When she entered the office, she was surprised to see the same young man who was walking among them earlier in the day. She was very sad to see that he had been caught. The SS started the interrogation. Ica was instructed in German as to which questions to ask in Hungarian and to translate the answers into German. "Who are you? Where did you come from? What is your name? Who sent you? What is your plan?" These were some of the many questions that she had to ask. The young man did not say a word. He stared at Ica the entire time with piercing eyes.

When she returned to the barrack, she felt sick and could not stop crying.

This was not an easy task for such a gentle and kind-hearted person. There was nothing that she could have done for the young and courageous spy. For the rest of her life she never forgot him.

Winter was approaching and they had no undergarments — just the one piece of ragged clothing they wore. They were very cold. Outside of the factory one day they found empty cement bags that had been thrown away. Ica picked up a bag and pulled it over her body. Others did the same. Through the long, snowy winter the women wore cement bags under their clothing to keep the cold out.

One night Ica was awakened and handed a piece of paper. She was told to deliver the message to another building. While she was outside delivering the message, the sirens went off during the night, and the lights were immediately turned off in the entire camp.

It was very dark outside. The starless black sky offered no light and she could not see where she was going. She was trying to feel her way in the dark, taking small steps one after another, and suddenly she fell into a large ditch full of metal scraps. It was deep and she was unable to climb out of it. She kept calling for help in German until finally, after a long time, the SS supervisor Kreiner walked by and heard the call.

"*Wer ist dort?*" ('Who is there?') Kreiner asked.

"*Ein häftling*" ('A prisoner'), she responded.

To Ica's surprise he lowered a thick rope and pulled her out. She returned to the barrack cold and tired, hoping to catch a little sleep before it was time to get up at dawn.

An Act of Resistance

Conditions continued to be as harsh in Hessisch Lichtenau as they were in Auschwitz. Food portions were scarce, and the women were starving. The severe hunger and malnutrition were an enormous threat to their lives. Starvation claimed many lives.

In the evenings after they returned from the factory, they often talked about food. It was comforting to recall happier times when food was abundant. Talking about food and remembering beloved family dishes gave them hope and a will to live. It was essential for their survival.

Ica and her fellow inmates talked about all the wonderful foods they had prepared and eaten at home. The women shared favorite recipes for appetizers and main dishes, but most of all they shared recipes for exquisite Austro-Hungarian pastries.

Ica wanted to write down and keep the recipes her fellow prisoners shared with her. She was fully aware that writing was very risky and knew that her life could be in danger if the recipes were discovered. In spite of the danger, she resolved to find paper and a pen or pencil.

The cleaning duties on the premises of the factory proved to be advantageous for her. One day she found a very small pencil on the floor of the factory. She still needed paper to write on. When she was cleaning in the factory, she saw a large stack of paper inside the trash basket! When the guards were not looking, she quickly took them out of the trash basket and hid them.

They were printed forms in German on one side. The forms were intended to be filled out indicating the type of ammunition and quantity, but were thrown away without being used. Among the tossed-out papers were also preprinted memos, access passes, discharge bills, shift inventories and prisoner correspondence templates. The back sides were blank and suitable for writing.

The recipes were written in Hungarian and mostly by Ica. She often wrote the name of the person who provided the recipe. Some of the recipes only have the first name of the person — perhaps because they knew each other well. Other recipes have the full name and, in a few instances, even the name of the town or city the person came from.

From the time they arrived at Hessisch Lichtenau in August 1944 until spring 1945 when the camp was evacuated, Ica wrote and collected over 600 recipes!

In the concentration camp Ica met three women from the Böhm family who were from Budapest and Miskolc. One was the wife of an engineer, and the other two were wives of factory owners. The Böhm family had planned to leave Hungary before the war and emigrate to Australia, where they dreamed of opening a café serving Hungarian pastries. They learned many great recipes from the famous *Gerbeaud Cukrászda* in Budapest. Ever since its establishment in 1858, Café Gerbeaud has been known as one of the best places for pastry in all of Budapest.[48] The Böhm family paid a substantial amount of money to buy the recipes in preparation for starting their own business, and they knew many of the recipes by heart.

Unfortunately, the Böhm family did not make it out of Hungary in time. They were deported and were together with Ica in both Auschwitz-Birkenau and Hessisch Lichtenau. They shared recipes with Ica as did many other women.

The recipes Ica wrote and collected had to be hidden from the SS guards and from the *kapo*, or she would be shot by the SS. She made a pouch from a piece of fabric torn from the seams of her long summer coat. She hid the recipes in this pouch, which she tied to the inside of her coat. She had lost a lot of weight due to starvation, and the coat was large on her small body. She was able to hide the pouch without it being noticed.

Block inspections were conducted frequently and each barrack was carefully inspected for extra food or any other items that they were not permitted to have. The responsibility of the *kapo* was to ensure that rules were followed in the barracks and during the forced labor at the munitions factory. Ica had to be very careful not to be discovered with the recipes and a pencil in her possession.

Death March

The Germans knew that they were losing the war. An older Nazi who was in charge of distributing the "coffee" felt sorry for the women seeing how much they suffered, and toward the end of the war he began to share bits and pieces of news with them. One day he whispered to Ica and her friends, "Don't worry. The Americans are coming. Soon you will be free."

The Allied troops were approaching the area and gunfire could be heard from not too far away. Hitler gave orders to gas all the remaining Jews. The Nazis decided to evacuate the camp and take the women to the gas chamber of the Theresienstadt concentration camp in Terezín, Czechoslovakia (now the Czech Republic). The gas chamber was built there toward the end of the war.

Hessisch Lichtenau, the subcamp of Buchenwald, was evacuated on March 29, 1945. Once again the women were put on freight trains. The train made numerous stops over several days. The Americans were already nearby, and due to frequent bombings, continuing to transport the women by train became out of the question.

In Leipzig they stayed overnight in a vacant *Hitler-Jugend* (Hitler Youth) building. The Allies did not know that the building had been evacuated by the Nazis and was instead being occupied by the women, and consequently the Allies started to bomb it during the night. As the Allies shot phosphorous and dropped magnesium flare bombs to illuminate the building and started to fly lower with their airplanes, they were surprised to see women running out of the building.

Immediately they stopped the bombing, but part of the building was already in flames. A few women died, but the majority of them escaped by running out of the building in the middle of the night.

Ica ran outside with the others, but then realized she had forgotten the pouch with the recipes inside the building.

"My recipes! I forgot my recipes!" She turned around and ran back to rescue her precious recipe collection.

Her sister and others cried out to her, "Ica, what are you doing? Don't go back inside!"

But she did not listen, exclaiming to them, "I have to get my recipes," and she ran back into the burning building.

The following morning the SS guards took the women from Leipzig on a forced death march. They marched over long distances under very harsh conditions. Many prisoners were shot during the death march. The women were very weak from exhaustion and starvation. They no longer received daily rations and food was even scarcer. They were taken through fields and woods, and those who could not keep up and lagged behind were immediately shot.

Under these extremely harsh conditions, Ica still found an inner drive to survive. She was determined to help her younger sister, who had turned 17 years old in the concentration camp. There were times when Ica physically supported her sister on the long march.

During the death march they occasionally stopped for a short rest. On one of the rest stops, they overheard someone calling, "Ica, hurry! Vera fainted." Ica knew that her cousin Vera must have fainted from hunger and she gave her cousin the piece of bread that Ica had saved for herself for later. Her cousin ate the bread and felt better. Ica remembered that some of the women were asking her, "And who will give you food when you get sick and faint?" Under these horrific conditions not everyone was willing to share.

Not far from Wurzen in Germany was a cheese factory. Ica recalled that the factory threw out rotten cheese. The women were very happy that the SS guards allowed them to eat the spoiled cheese.

They were near Wurzen on this death march when the SS guards took a rest stop with the women at a farm. The farmer agreed to cook potatoes for them. A Hungarian woman by the name of Piri could not wait any longer to eat, and while the potatoes were still cooking, she grabbed a hot potato from the pot. She was immediately shot by the SS guard. Piri lost her life only days before the women were liberated. Piri had shared a few recipes with Ica, and one of the recipes has been translated into English at the end of this book.

The Americans were approaching from one side at the same time the Soviets were coming from the other side. So as not to get caught, the camp commander and a few of the SS guards deserted the transport. The remaining SS guards, who were determined to gas the women in Theresienstadt, continued marching them toward the Czech border. By this time they marched the women mostly during the night, hoping to avoid detection by the Allies.

The remaining SS guards realized that they would not make it to Theresienstadt. The Allies were getting too close to them. They began to fear for their own lives and started to ponder who to give themselves up to, the Americans or the Soviets. More and more SS continued to abandon the transport of women and were escaping to save their own lives.

One day the women found themselves all alone without the SS guards. On this day, the death march that began two weeks before came to an end in Wurzen, about 26 kilometers (16 miles) from Leipzig.

Liberated at Last

hen the women realized that they were alone and were no longer supervised by the SS guards, they began to disperse on their own. They formed small groups and slowly started to walk toward the Czech border, hoping to make it to their hometowns. The war was over and they were eager to go home.

Ica and Babi together with their friends Rózsi Breitbart and Magda Fischer joined a group led by Mrs. Lea Paskusz. Mrs. Paskusz was an older religious lady who came from a family of many generations of rabbis. She survived together with her daughter, Kornélia.

In Auschwitz Mrs. Paskusz had secretly conducted Friday evening Shabbat* services. Several women from various barracks gathered around Mrs. Paskusz on Friday evenings outside of one of the barracks for a brief Shabbat service, so as not to attract the attention of the SS guards. Mrs. Paskusz said a prayer over two unlit candle stubs and ended by blessing everyone before they dispersed and returned to their barracks.

Religious services were forbidden by the Nazis, but Jews engaged in various forms of defiance during the Holocaust.[49] In this case it was spiritual resistance,

---

* Shabbat is the Jewish day of rest, which begins at sunset every Friday and lasts until sundown every Saturday. Before sunset begins on Friday evenings, traditionally the woman of the household lights Shabbat candles and recites a blessing. The family gathers around the dinner table and the man of the household recites the Kiddush, a prayer over wine sanctifying the Shabbat. Then follows the prayer for eating bread, which is recited over two loaves of challah, a braided bread. A festive, leisurely family dinner follows.

having clandestine religious observances every week. Prayer helped sustain morale, reaffirmed their cultural and religious identity and provided spiritual comfort. Individuals attempted to maintain their humanity and integrity in spite of Nazi attempts to dehumanize and degrade them.

The small group of about ten women led by Mrs. Paskusz continued walking and eventually stopped in a barn to rest. They were hoping to get a little food from the farmer, but were told to leave immediately. They kept walking during the day and rested in the cornfields at night. One night a group of *Wehrmacht* soldiers (German armed forces) came upon them, and when they realized who they were, they told them which direction to go so that they would not run into the SS who were heading in their direction and would have undoubtedly killed them. These soldiers were disillusioned after losing the war and they wanted to get home to their families. While trudging along at night, the women sometimes tripped over dead people or dead horses.

Early one morning, they came upon a stable. The farmer told them that they could not stay there, but he pointed out which direction they should go in to meet up with British soldiers. He gave them a white piece of cloth. Mrs. Paskusz walked at the head of the group and was holding up the white cloth that the farmer had given them. After walking for a while, they arrived at a place where they had to cross over the river on a narrow wooden board because the bridge had been damaged.

Ica had a phobia of heights and crossing on a narrow bridge over the water scared her.

"Mrs. Paskusz, I cannot cross over this narrow board. I will stay here," she said.

Mrs. Paskusz would not hear of leaving her behind.

"No, you will not stay behind! I want you to come up to the front of the line and walk behind me and repeat the words of the following prayer after me!" she replied.

Then Mrs. Paskusz recited the Priestly Blessing in Hebrew (translated in English[50]) as they crossed the river on the narrow board:

May God bless you and safeguard you.
May God make his face shine upon you and be gracious to you.
May God show you kindness and establish peace for you.

Everyone crossed safely to the other side, including Ica. Mrs. Paskusz liked her. "You should always say this prayer and God will help you," she told her. Ica often said this prayer for the remainder of her life.

Suddenly they saw an American jeep approaching near Riesa or Dahlen in Germany. The women were overjoyed to see them. The jeep came to a stop in front of them and four American soldiers stepped out. One soldier was from Ohio and spoke a little German. Ica explained to him in German who they were. They took the women to Wurzen, where they were liberated on April 25, 1945.[51]

In Wurzen, after an American doctor checked them out, they were required to stay and recuperate for a few weeks. The doctor advised them to eat slowly and only very small portions. They received a change of clean clothes. Although Ica and Babi were extremely thin, both sisters were very fortunate that they remained healthy and free of disease. Tuberculosis, typhus, dysentery and other serious diseases were very common among the prisoners.

Journey Home

After recuperation, the two sisters began their journey back home. Together with a small group of women they walked from Wurzen toward the Czech border. Germany suffered heavy losses and many cities were severely damaged from bombing. There was no public transportation available and walking was the only option for them. They stopped to rest often and it took them weeks to walk to their destination.

They went through the German city of Dresden, which had been heavily bombed before the end of World War II by the British and Americans.[52] Ica recalled the city of Dresden being in ruins; some buildings were standing as empty shells. She also saw buildings sliced in half with perfect precision.

They finally arrived at the Czech border and were greeted by the train dispatcher of a small Czech town, the name of which Ica could not remember. The dispatcher and his colleague saluted the women and welcomed them back. They called them heroes and few of the women began to cry. It had been a long time since they had been treated with respect. The two train station employees invited them inside their office, where they offered the women food and drink.

In this small Czech town they boarded the train — this time a passenger train — and they continued their journey back to Plešivec. The survivors had no money to buy train tickets and the transportation was provided for free to them. Ica and Babi arrived at their hometown at the end of July 1945.

Returning to their hometown of Plešivec was very sad. The two sisters walked home from the train station. When they arrived at their family house in the center of the town, nothing was the same. Their parents had been killed. Their house was empty. All their possessions had been stolen. A desk and a single bed were all that remained in their large two-story house.

Their father's elegant carriage was still standing in the covered inner courtyard. The two sisters had nothing except the clothes they were wearing. They didn't even have a photograph of their parents. They would have to start life all over again.

Injustice After the Holocaust

Mr. Homoly, a former guard in the Plešivec ghetto, approached Ica after the war to inquire about Marika. "Please tell me what happened to that beautiful little girl from Jelšava," he asked. "She was murdered in Auschwitz. Her fate was the same as the fate of all the young children," Ica said sadly.

As survivors began to return home they were often treated with hostility from the non-Jewish population. Jewish properties had been taken by the local people, and they feared that the Jews would demand that their property and belongings be returned.

Mr. Becske had worked for Ica's father before the war. Whenever there was a funeral, Mr. Becske would bring his two horses to pull the family's elegant black hearse to the cemetery. He was a decent man and when he saw that Ica had returned after the war, Mr. Becske told her that the Kondás family had moved into her family's house during the war. Apparently as soon as Mr. Kondás heard that the two sisters survived and were on their way back, he hired a few people and loaded up four horse-drawn carriages with all of Ica's family's belongings. He moved across the border to a town called Putnok in Hungary. Czechoslovakia had been restored in the spring of 1945 and Plešivec was once again part of Czechoslovakia.[53] At that time Ica's official name changed from Ilona to Elena.

Ica received permission to travel to Hungary. She took the train to Putnok and stopped at the police station. She asked to be escorted by a police officer

to the home of the Kondás family. When they got there, Mrs. Kondás opened
the door. When she saw Ica, she wanted to close the door, but Ica pushed it
open and stepped inside. Mrs. Kondás was alone at home. Inside the house Ica
immediately recognized many items that had belonged to her family. Mr. Kondás
had discovered the hiding place after the family's house was bombed during the
war and had stolen everything. The bedding and the towels had Ica's monogram
on it. "All these are mine! They belong to me and my sister," Ica said. The woman
did not say a word, just stood silently staring at Ica.

Ica left and returned to the police station. She reported the theft to the
chief of police. He told her that she had no permission to take anything across
the border. Mr. Kondás was a Hungarian citizen and Ica was Czechoslovak. The
Hungarian chief of police protected Mr. Kondás and Ica had no right to reclaim
the belongings that he had stolen from her family. Consequently, they had no
pots for cooking, no bedding or towels and no clothes to wear — nothing but an
empty house.

Ica and Babi each had only the dress they had received from the American
soldiers when they were liberated, and they had no money to buy anything. A
local woman talked to Ica.

"Icuka, the Puskás family has most of your clothes. Their daughter Cili is
wearing your dresses. Why don't you ask for a few dresses back?" she suggested.
Ica thought about it and the next day she went to the home of Mrs. Puskás and
politely inquired about the situation.

She said, "Mrs. Puskás, please forgive me for asking, but I heard that your
daughter Cili has most of my clothes. Please return a few pieces to me because
I just came back from the concentration camp and I have no clothes to wear."
The woman looked at Ica and became very angry.

"You filthy, rotten Jews! I wish that none of you had returned," she yelled.
When Ica heard those terrible words, she felt a stabbing pain inside her and a
surge of anger. She grabbed the much taller woman and pushed her down on the
sofa, casting whatever blows she could. Then, she abruptly left for home.

Ica was shocked by the degree of anger that had suddenly welled up inside
her toward this woman. Since she had never behaved like this before, she asked

herself what the cause of this was. She realized that hearing those terribly hateful words at so painful a time for her — when she was grieving the murder of her dear parents — incited this unexpected display of anger and the resulting behavior. What also surprised Ica was her own strength, how she managed to overpower a taller and much stronger woman. Ica had not yet fully recovered from malnutrition and was still very thin after more than a year of starvation in Auschwitz and the subcamp of Buchenwald. She thought of her parents, two kind and good people, who always helped those who were in need. They did not deserve to die. None of them deserved it.

After the incident Ica went home and was very upset. It was a Friday afternoon and she was expected to meet Mr. Kóth for dinner in the Kosher Kitchen. Kóth *bácsi* (literally 'uncle' — used as a respectful term to address an older man) was an older gentleman who had miraculously survived. He was a very good friend of her parents. Ica did not go. She stayed at home crying. Kóth *bácsi* was very worried when she didn't show up and sent somebody to get her. That person talked to her and convinced her to go. When Ica arrived at the restaurant, Kóth *bácsi* said, "My dear child, what happened? Where were you? We have been waiting for you." Ica told him the story.

Mrs. Puskás had scratches from the incident and went to see the doctor. When asked, she told the doctor what had happened. The doctor was curious about Ica and he inquired about her from others. One day the doctor stopped by to visit her and he introduced himself.

"I heard very good things about you, but forgive me for asking, did you really beat up Mrs. Puskás?" he asked.

"Yes, I did," Ica replied. She explained to the doctor what had happened and told him about the anger she felt hearing those terrible words after losing her parents.

Mrs. Puskás filed a lawsuit. Ica phoned her cousin Lenke in Tisovec, who was a few years older than Ica and was like a mother to her. Ica told her what happened.

"I am happy you did it and I will pay all the expenses. I am very proud of you that you stood up against an antisemite," she said.

Dr. Botto was the presiding judge. Ica was ordered to pay a fine of 500 Czechoslovak *koruna* and her cousin Lenke paid it. Although the judge asked them to shake hands, Ica refused. When she was leaving, Dr. Botto followed her outside. He wanted to know if she was satisfied with the outcome.

Ica's beautiful Petrof piano, given to her by her parents, was stolen during the war. After the war she found out that Mr. Balogh, a judge in Jelšava, had her piano. She wanted the piano back and traveled to Jelšava to see Mr. Balogh. He told her that he had bought the piano from Pista, a gypsy man, and he would return it to her if she would pay back the thousands of Czechoslovak *koruna* he had paid for it.

"Do you suggest that I pay for it when it belongs to me?" asked Ica.
He refused to give back the piano, and Ica decided to sue Mr. Balogh.

During the court hearing he swore to the judge that he had paid for the piano. Ica lost the lawsuit and the piano was never returned to her. The presiding judge was again Dr. Botto. Afterward he wanted to talk to Ica and followed her to the hallway. Dr. Botto told her that he was fully aware that this piano belonged to her. He remembered that her father had bought this piano for her from Mr. Smolka. Dr. Botto explained that he had often played on this piano when it still belonged to Mr. Smolka. He expressed his regrets that there was nothing he could do about returning it to her.

Ica was very disappointed with the outcome and all the injustices she faced trying to reclaim the possessions that were stolen from her. She had the right to demand that her family's possessions be returned to her and her sister. She did what she felt was right by trying to get at least some of the possessions back. Amazingly, she did not display anger or bitterness. Even if she was not satisfied with the court ruling, she accepted it, looked ahead and lived her life as best as she possibly could.

Start Life Anew

I ca and Babi had lost so much. They had lost their parents, many of their families and friends, and all of their possessions. They had to find a way to support themselves.

Their cousins Lenke and Ella were in hiding in the mountains and villages during the war. They were hiding with their elderly mother and Ella's infant daughter, Katka, while Ella's husband, Menhard, made a decision to join the partisans. After the war Lenke resumed working as a pharmacist. Her younger sister, Ella, was close in age to Ica, and the two of them had attended school together in Brno. They had a close relationship throughout their lives. These two sisters, Lenke and Ella, were very helpful to Ica and Babi.

There were others who were kind and wanted to help. A large paper industry and a pulp mill were located in Gemerská Hôrka, only 3 kilometers from Plešivec. The management of the factory knew the Kellner family well and they reached out to Ica and offered her the task of distributing rations to the factory employees. She accepted the offer and was paid. This enabled her to earn a little extra money for a few years.

She opened a textile business located on the ground floor of the Kellner family house. Upstairs were the living quarters for Ica and Babi, the same as it had been for their parents before the war. Mr. Zahoranský, the president of the Communist Party who worked in the city hall in Rožňava, helped Ica to get a permit to open her own store. He was also instrumental in speeding up the process so she could open the store much sooner.

In addition to the textile business, Ica decided to sell caskets — the same as her father had done in the past.* Ica's father had bought the caskets from Mr. Mičinsky in Jelšava. They had a very good business relationship that spanned over many years. Mr. Mičinsky knew and trusted her family and now wanted to help her. He did not take money in advance and suggested that Ica pick out different kinds and sizes of caskets and take them on consignment. She would pay only when she sold them. Ica's business was going well. She enjoyed what she was doing and excelled at it.

---

* The elegant black hearse remained in the covered courtyard of the family house after the war. I don't recall the hearse ever being used during my childhood, except when my cousin Robi and I played on it, hopping on and off the carriage, which was being pulled by imaginary horses.

Ica and Ernő Meet

Ica and Ernő met after the war. His family name had changed from Kaufmann to Kalina. Unbeknownst to the other, after the war each had started a textile business, Ica in Plešivec and Ernő in Jelšava.

Before World War II, Ernő had owned a successful business with his father. The store was founded by his father in early 1900. At the war's end Ernő returned home, stopped in his store and asked that the store be given back to him. Mr. Kristof, who had taken over the store without any compensation to the family, refused to give it back to him. Mr. Kristof said that the store belonged to him because he worked there and took care of it for about a year after the Jews were taken away. Ernő was a good-natured person who did not like to argue. He accepted the few pieces of merchandise the man offered him and opened up his own textile store.

Ica traveled to Jelšava to purchase the caskets for her business, and on one of those trips, she stopped in Ernő's store to inquire about his sister, Vali. Ica and Vali had been together in the Plešivec ghetto and in Auschwitz. It was Vali, who carried Ernő's daughter, Marika, in her arms in Auschwitz-Birkenau. During selections she was asked by Mengele if she was the mother of the child. When she replied, "No. I am her aunt," she was ordered to give the child back to Irénke. This was the last time that Vali saw little Marika. Mother and child were immediately sent to the gas chamber.

Ica stopped by to visit Vali in the store on another day, and it was then that she met Ernő for the first time. They talked for a while and had a nice conversation. After this initial meeting they often ran into each other on the train when traveling on business trips to buy merchandise for their stores. On those occasions, they sat together and talked. Ica told Ernő how she had met his wife and young daughter in the ghetto.

Whenever Ica traveled on business to Jelšava, she always stopped to visit her cousin Vera and Vera's husband Imre Foltýn. Vera was together with Ica and Babi in both Auschwitz and Hessisch-Lichtenau. Imre asked her one day to make *krémes* for them, well-known Hungarian napoleons.[54] Vera did not have eggs at home, so Imre suggested that Ica go with him to buy eggs on the Muránska *ulica*. Ernő lived on this street and Imre was secretly hoping that they would see him. As luck would have it, they indeed did meet him on the street.

"Ernő, do you like *krémes*? Because Ica makes the best *krémes*," Imre asked him.

To his surprise, Ernő said, "I don't like *krémes*."
It was too rich for his taste. Imre was trying to make a match between the two.

One day Ica and Ernő ran into each other on the streets of Jelšava. He greeted her and politely asked if he could walk her to where she was going. During the walk they talked for a while and afterward he proposed to her. He told her that he liked her very much and would like to marry her.

Ica said, "You are a nice, sympathetic person, but I don't want to get married." She had already turned down a few marriage proposals before. Ernő's feelings were hurt.

"Icuka, I wish you good luck, all the best and lots of happiness to you. Goodbye," he said politely and left.
Ica was very upset and returned to her cousin's house and started to cry. Immediately, Imre sensed what must have happened.

"What is the matter? Did you turn down Ernő? Don't worry. He will find someone very soon," he told her.

"I am not worried about it. I just did not mean to hurt him, and I know that I did because right away he said goodbye and left," she replied.

The next time they happened to be traveling on a business trip at the same time, Ernő tried to avoid Ica on the train. When he saw her from afar, he turned around and went in the opposite direction. Other times he even got off the train when it was slowing down, right before it pulled into the station, so that he did not have to walk with her from the train station.

One Sunday afternoon, May or June 1947, Ica traveled again to Jelšava. She stopped by to visit Vera and Imre, but they were not at home. She was walking away from her cousin's house when suddenly she saw Ernő coming toward her on the street. By the time he noticed Ica, it was too late for him to avoid her, and he politely greeted her.

She asked him if he happened to know where Vera and Imre were, because she did not find them at home.

"Yes, they are visiting my brother and sister-in-law," he replied. Ernő invited her to his brother's house. She was hesitant to go because she did not know Sanyi's second wife, Lili, well, but Ernő convinced her to go.

They walked up the stairs to his brother's house, and besides seeing Vera and Imre there, they discovered Ica's cousin, Ella, from Tisovec, was also visiting. They were very happy to see Ica and Ernő together. This is what the families had hoped for since the war had ended.

Both families felt that the two had a lot in common, the same values and beliefs and very similar family backgrounds. They hoped Ica and Ernő could have a life together after their tragic losses.

Sanyi did not waste too much time.

"I have a proposition, now that we are all together. Let's have an engagement for Ica and Ernő," he announced. Ernő looked at Ica and asked her if she wanted to go to the adjacent room and talk.

Once they were alone, he proposed to her once again saying, "Icuka, if you change your mind, I am willing to marry you even though you turned me down once before."

This time, she said, "Yes."

They returned to the others and made the announcement. Everyone was very happy for them. They felt it was a perfect match. Then the housekeeper Ancsa *néni* (literally 'aunt' — used as a respectful term to address an older woman), who was familiar with Jewish customs, ran to the kitchen, got a plate and threw it on the floor.* When the plate was broken, everyone called out "*Mazel-Tov!*"

On that Sunday afternoon, there was an engagement party without any advance planning. They had plenty of pastries and drinks to celebrate.

Ica and Ernő on their honeymoon (1947). From Moreimi family archives.

Meanwhile Babi had a feeling something was going on. She tried to phone her cousin Vera, but there was no answer. She decided to phone Sanyi's house and said that she was looking for Ica. They told her that Ica had just gotten engaged. Babi was very happy to hear that Ica finally decided to get married.

After they got engaged, Ernő visited Ica often, traveling by train from Jelšava to Plešivec. As it was the custom in many homes, Ica always had a platter of freshly baked pastries, including *linzer*, *rétes* (strudel), *almás pitte* (apple pastry), a variety of *kuchen* (yeast coffee cakes), plain or filled with cinnamon and sugar, walnuts or chocolate, and much more.

Ica loved to bake, and it did not take her long to bake more pastries. If visitors stopped by on any day, she always had pastries to offer with a cup of coffee, a latte or a strong espresso.

Often by the time Babi got home from work, most of the pastries were gone. One day, she found the entire platter empty. She would often say, "Ernő must have been here visiting again because all the pastries are gone."

Ica and Ernő were married in September 1947. Léderer *bácsi*, who was a good friend of Ernő's father, offered to have the wedding in his house in Šafárikovo (Tornalja) amidst his beautiful indoor palm trees. His wife prepared a nice dinner for the guests. It was a very small wedding with only a few relatives and friends. After the wedding Ernő moved to Plešivec and they lived in the Kellner family house.

Some months later they shared the news that Ica was pregnant. Ernő's sister, Margo, phoned to tell them how very happy she was.

"I heard that you are pregnant, Ica. I am very happy for both of you. I hope you will have a daughter. I know that Ernő would be so happy to have a daughter," she told Ica.

She dearly loved her brother and thought about the loss of his first daughter. After a difficult labor, my parents welcomed me, their daughter.

---

*The Jewish custom of breaking a plate symbolizes the seriousness of their commitment to each other and the permanence of the marriage. Just as breaking the plate is considered final, so too is the engagement considered final and not easily terminated. It also tempers the intense joy of the occasion. Even in a moment of such great joy, we are asked to remember that there is still pain and suffering in the world and that we have a responsibility to help relieve some of that suffering.

ARTIFACTS

Prisoner number assigned to and worn by Ica in the Hessisch Lichtenau forced labor camp, a subcamp of Buchenwald, in Germany. Donated to the United States Holocaust Memorial Museum.

Identification pin given to Ica while imprisoned in the Hessisch Lichtenau forced labor camp. She received the pin because she worked as a translator and messenger in the camp. Donated to the United States Holocaust Memorial Museum

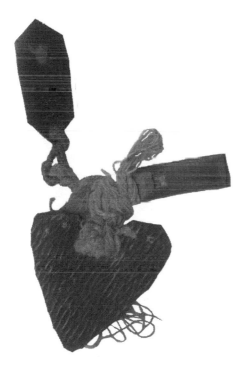

A leather charm on the wooden clogs issued to Ica in the Auschwitz-Birkenau concentration camp in Poland. Donated to the United States Holocaust Memorial Museum.

PART TWO

Living with Holocaust Survivor Parents

I n spite of my parents' horrific experiences during the Holocaust, I grew up in a happy home with a family that was very close and affectionate. My parents were doting, unselfish and devoted.

My mother still sang and played the piano, which my parents bought for me a few years after the war, but sometimes playing evoked nostalgic memories for her. After playing two or three pieces on the piano and singing, she would abruptly stop and look at my father and me with a smile that expressed sadness and pain.

Our home was always filled with lots of love, laughter and music — and food. Because they were deprived of food during the Holocaust, my mother made sure that we always had plenty of food and that it was of the best quality.

I remember that the pantry next to our kitchen had shelves on both sides all the way up to the tall ceiling and was replete with glass jars of food like homemade jams, fruit syrups and preserves, pickles and pickled vegetables, and many other items to last through the winter. My mother was a very good cook and our meals consisted of a variety of chicken dishes, veal, roasted duck or goose, turkey and fish. Homemade bread was a very important staple in our home, and we all liked bread, but especially my mother. Bread was almost holy to her. If she dropped a piece, she picked it up and kissed it. My parents continued to have an abundance of food throughout the remainder of their lives.

Most of my parents' friends were survivors of the concentration camps and forced labor. A few had survived while in hiding. They had all lost loved ones in the war. When my parents got together with their friends, I usually played in the background and often overheard parts of their conversations. Mostly the conversations were inconsequential to me, but I became attentive when I overheard them discussing the fate of the family members they had lost or recalling their own experiences during the war. Those times I saw deep sadness and pain on their faces and often tears, and I always wanted to know more.

Seeing my parents' deep hurt was painful for me, but I suppressed the pain I felt. Since I was a child, I was very protective of them and felt that I must always be on my best behavior and not cause any trouble. They had already experienced too much pain in their life, and I was careful not to cause any more.

At an early age I began to ask my parents questions. Not having grandparents, unlike my Christian friends, and overhearing bits and pieces of stories prompted me to ask many questions. My questions were always answered by my parents truthfully and appropriately for my age. My parents gave me simple answers when I was young, so as not to scare me. It was important to my parents to tell the truth. I was never silenced or dismissed.

Most survivors did not talk about the Holocaust to their children to protect them.[55] My parents spoke about their experiences and were never silent about their past. My mother was very outgoing and sociable. She thrived on storytelling and that included also sharing stories about her Holocaust experiences.

But most importantly, my parents attempted to return to a life of normalcy and to create a safe, nurturing and loving environment for me. They were overprotective but not excessively so. They were both resilient and overcame their negative experiences of tragedy and suffering. They had each other, and they had me.

Behind the Iron Curtain

C zechoslovakia was a strong democratic country in Central Europe before World War II. After the war, attempts were made to rebuild the country.[56] However, in February 1948, the Communist Party under Soviet influence seized complete power. This was the start of the Communist totalitarian regime that lasted until the Velvet Revolution of 1989. This prompted a wave of nationalization and companies, industries and banks were seized and nationalized by the Communist regime. Agriculture was collectivized, and small private retail businesses and services were confiscated and became the property of the state.

After they married, my parents, Ica and Ernő, combined their two businesses into one. The business was going well and they worked there together. However, their livelihood was taken away from them once again, this time under the communist regime. My parents lost their business in the early 1950s. My father suffered a nervous breakdown. There was so much loss in his life. While he was hospitalized, my mother had to take care of me on her own. He fully recovered thanks to the help of my strong and devoted mother.

My parents were once again unemployed. They both needed to work to support their family of three. My father found a position in finance and worked as a bookkeeper in the offices of the large Psychiatric Hospital in Plešivec, established in the late 1800s by Samuel Blum.[57] My father was good with numbers and was organized and detail oriented. My mother managed a florist shop. The store was located on the street level of our house that once belonged to my grandparents, and we shared the house with my aunt. My mother knew very little about plants and flowers, had never even gardened before, but she was willing to learn.

The economy went steadily downhill under the Communist regime.[58] My parents lived from paycheck to paycheck. Basic human rights were again suppressed. Censorship became law. Media was controlled by the government and religious practices were discouraged. People could not express disapproval of the regime and were afraid to speak openly. My family did not get involved in politics.

We left Plešivec in the early 1960s and moved to Košice, a city in eastern Czechoslovakia, which is now Slovakia, where I attended and graduated from Economic School Košice, the second largest city in Slovakia after Bratislava, had synagogues and an active Jewish community with the Jewish population numbering around 1,300. This was a huge decline from the 1930s when over 11,000 Jews had lived in Košice. Seventy percent of Košice Jews were murdered in Auschwitz-Birkenau, among them my father's first cousin Boriska Lieberman and her daughter. Today the Jewish population in Košice consists of only a few hundred people.[59]

It was not until "Prague Spring," beginning in January 1968, under the leadership of Alexander Dubček, the secretary of the Communist Party, that there was an attempt to create a more humane version of socialism. Democratization was taking place and more freedom was granted to the citizens. Restrictions on the media, speech and travel were slowly being lifted. These changes were taking place in the spring; therefore, it became known as the Prague Spring.[60]

The Soviet Union viewed this reform as a threat. On August 21, 1968, thousands of Soviet troops and tanks along with the Warsaw Pact member countries invaded Czechoslovakia, ending the process called the Prague Spring.

Immigrating to USA

After the invasion, the new Czechoslovak government, backed by the Soviet Union, instituted stricter censorship. Hopes of normalization and freedom enjoyed during the Prague Spring were shattered. A large wave of emigration, forced by the political situation, followed the Soviet invasion. An estimated 70,000 fled Czechoslovakia immediately, with about 300,000 leaving in total.[61]

We witnessed many friends and acquaintances leaving the country, and both my father and I wanted to leave. My father's three sisters and their families had already moved to the United States and were living in Cleveland. They were hoping that my parents and I would join them. For my mother, it was very difficult to leave her sister. How could she leave her sister, she would ask, when they had survived Auschwitz together, where she cared for and protected her? She always felt a strong sense of responsibility toward her younger sister, especially after their parents were murdered. They were very close their entire lives.

I yearned for a better future and wanted to live in a democracy, where there was freedom of speech and religion and everyone was entitled to vote. I knew that it was up to me to make the first step. It was spring 1969 when I applied for a visa to England. Though it was difficult for me to leave my parents, I knew that it would be even more difficult for them. But in my heart I knew that when I left, they would follow.

I received a visa for England and left Czechoslovakia exactly one year and one day after the Soviet invasion. After spending a few weeks in England, I traveled to France and spent a few months in Paris, where I waited for my US visa. I arrived in Cleveland, Ohio, to join my family, most of whom I did not know. They welcomed me with open arms and lots of love. I moved in with my aunt Margo. My parents applied for their visas and waited impatiently to get them. They left Czechoslovakia and joined me in Cleveland in spring 1971, twenty-one months after I left. It was a joyful reunion. They were not only reuniting with me, but also with the three sisters, along with their families, whom my father had not seen for so many years.

It was not easy for my parents to immigrate and start new lives at the ages of 59 and 62. Although both my parents were fluent in Czechoslovak, Hungarian and German, they did not speak English. They had to learn a new language and find work. My mother worked at Control Data and was considered a very good employee. My father worked at a major book wholesaler, The Bookmen, where during breaks he began to read books in English. He learned to read and write and to some extent speak English. My parents worked for years and retired at a later age. Despite the many challenges that they faced as immigrants, they had many very happy years in the United States.

My aunt Babi visiting us in the USA (1977). From Moreimi family archives.

Ica's Sister Babi

After the war my aunt Babi found employment as an administrative clerk in the local postal services, where she worked for many years. She got married in her early twenties to a young man, Laci, who resided in Plešivec. They had a son, Robi, who was four years younger than me. Ica and Babi continued to live together with their husbands and children, sharing the Kellner family home. Each family lived in one half of the house. We were very close, and a few years later they also left Plešivec and followed us to Košice. They remained living in Košice for the rest of their lives. My uncle Laci passed away in 2000.

We were very fortunate to be able to visit my aunt Babi during our trip to Europe in the spring of 2017. She was turning 90 years old in just two months and mentally she was still very sharp. It was very meaningful for our family to be able to spend some time with her.

For my three children, meeting my aunt was one of the highlights of the trip. They were delighted to meet her, as she reminded them of their beloved grandmother who had passed away six years before we had taken the trip. My children remembered some Hungarian from their grandparents, so while the youngest was somewhat able to follow the conversation, our oldest conversed in Hungarian, though not fluently. It was heartwarming and joyful to be together.

My aunt Babi passed away in December of the same year. My cousin Robi lives in Košice with his family.

Receiving a Torah

After the war, Plešivec no longer had a synagogue.[62] Many of the local Jewish community members perished during the Holocaust and those who survived did not want to continue living in Plešivec. They had many painful memories tied to this town, and they moved away or immigrated to another country.

My mother's cousin Pali Kellner, a pharmacist, took over the family pharmacy in Plešivec after the war and settled there with his wife, Magda, and son, Peter. They lived in Plešivec until about 1952, at which time they also moved away. After they moved, our family was the only Jewish family left in Plešivec.

An elderly, observant Catholic woman, Mrs. Balázs, entered my parents' store in late 1940s carrying a bundle in her arms. "I rescued this during the war. I know that it is sacred to the Jews and I want to give it back to you," she told my mother. To my mother's surprise she unwrapped a few rolled up Torah* scrolls and handed them to my mother.

She explained that during the war the synagogue in Plešivec was ransacked. The Torah scrolls were thrown out on the street, and when nobody was looking, she picked them up. "They got dirty because I picked them up from the street, but I wrapped them and hid them," she explained. My mother wanted to know where she had hidden them. Mrs. Balázs explained that after she wrapped the scrolls, she hid them inside a pile of straw under her pigs. She did not think that anyone would find them there. My mother was very touched receiving the Torah scrolls thanks to the courage and kindness of this woman. In return she gave Mrs. Balázs a few meters of fabric for some dresses.

The Torah scrolls, carefully wrapped by my mother in a white damask tablecloth, remained with my parents throughout their life and traveled with them from Czechoslovakia to the United States. The Torah scrolls consisted of six large fragments, each fragment measuring a few feet long. These fragments may have come from three different Torahs, each one incomplete.

My parents were in their 90s when they passed on the Torah fragments to me. The six Torah fragments have been professionally mounted and housed inside clear, protective acrylic covers. Today each of our three children have a framed Torah fragment in their home in memory of their grandparents and great-grandparents — and to never let the memory of the Holocaust be erased.

We gave one fragment to my cousin Robi, and another fragment we donated to our synagogue in memory of my parents, including with it the history of the Torah. It is a reminder that once there was a Jewish community in Plešivec.

My husband and I have the remaining Torah fragment in our home. These Torah fragments are very meaningful to me because they are a connection to my grandparents, whom I never knew.

---

* Torah, meaning teaching or law, is the most important document in Judaism and includes all Jewish laws and traditions. The Torah refers to the first Five Books of Moses or the Jewish bible. The words are handwritten on a parchment scroll kept in the ark of the synagogue, and the Torah is taken out and read in small sections during services.

Ica (aged 90) and Ernő (aged 93) in November 2002. From Moreimi family archives.

My Parents

My mother was a strong lady who got through many challenges in life. She was courageous, self-assured and very capable. She knew what she wanted in life and always remained true to herself, living with integrity, honesty and the values that were important to her. She was lively and animated, had a cheerful disposition and was pleasant and fun to be around. She loved life and people. She was kind and friendly with people from all walks of life.

My father was a very kind, sensitive and gentle person. He was pleasant, always with a smile on his face. He was very patient and polite and was a real old-school gentleman. I remember my father often kissing my mother's hand as a gesture of respect, admiration and devotion. He never raised his voice, not with my mother and not with me. I saw the affection between the two of them and their devotion to each other. Wherever they went, they always held hands.

They loved people and were also loved by many. It was much later, when they were older, that I realized how many lives had been touched over the years by their kindness.

My mother was 62 years old and my parents had lived in the United States for three years, when she announced to my husband and me that she had decided to get her driver's license. Neither of my parents had driven in Europe. This was to be her first time driving a car, and at that age! We were worried and assured them that we were happy to continue driving them to do grocery shopping and go anywhere else. My mother thanked us, but no, her mind was made up. She received her driver's license, and they bought a new car. She was a very good driver and drove the same car for over 20 years, until the car was no longer drivable.

When my parents did not have a car any longer, my husband, our oldest son or sometimes I always managed to take them wherever they needed to go. People truly liked them, and everywhere they went, they were greeted with much warmth. If it was the lady behind the cash register in one of the upscale grocery stores, or the nurses and the doctors during their medical appointments or the man in the car repair shop where they were loyal customers, they were treated exceptionally well. These were heartwarming experiences for me to see. So many people knew my parents by name and liked this older couple who were constant companions everywhere they went.

My mother loved to cook and even more she loved to bake. Although she did not eat many pastries, she liked seeing the pleasure on the faces of others who enjoyed the pastries she made. Everything was made from scratch and everything was superb. She could bake all kinds of Hungarian pastries, tortes, cookies and yeast cakes.

My parents had a loving, happy marriage for almost 60 years. They were inseparable. They were the role models for many of us: to me; my husband, Jack; our three children, Tommy, Mark and Corinne; and many of our friends. They were two remarkable people who in spite of hardships and suffering lived a happy life together.

My parents were an integral part of our lives. They were overjoyed and felt blessed becoming grandparents, and they developed a very special bond and closeness with their three grandchildren. Their unconditional and unwavering love for their family, and the love that they received in return from us, gave them a strong will to live. They lived a full life, and we were blessed to have them in our lives until they reached their late nineties.

A Fond Childhood Memory

One of many fond childhood memories I have is of watching my mother stretch out *rétes* (strudel), a flaky pastry dough. I must have been somewhere between five and seven years old, and I remember standing in the kitchen out of my mother's way, and observing.

She cleared off the round kitchen table and covered it with a white damask tablecloth. First, she sprinkled flour on the tablecloth, then she placed the dough in the middle of the table. The dough may have been approximately 12 inches long, 8 inches wide and about 1 to 2 inches thick. The dough preparation consisted of kneading the dough until it was elastic enough for making strudel. I watched my mother in awe as she patiently walked around and around the table, stretching the dough by gently lifting it and putting her hands underneath while slightly pulling it. I was fascinated to see that in a short time the dough was paper thin, covering the entire table and hanging down all around the edges just like the tablecloth did.

She prepared the fillings ahead of time, and there was always a variety. When the dough was stretched out, she added the filling, rolled up the dough and baked the strudel until it was medium brown in color. After it cooled a little, my mother sliced the strudel, placed the slices on a nice crystal platter and, with the help of a small sieve, sprinkled powdered sugar on top.

My father and I could hardly wait to taste the fresh, delicious and crispy strudels, deciding which one to try first. My favorite was the poppy seed, but

My mother and I at my son Mark's Bar-mitzvah (1992). All the pastries were made by my mother. From Moreimi family archives.

I also liked the walnut filling. My father's favorite was the apple strudel with cinnamon and the strudel filled with sour cherries. We both liked the farmer's cheese and raisins filling and had to have a piece of that one too.

My mother watched us with a smile on her face, so happy to see how much we enjoyed it. It was very gratifying to her to see how much family and friends enjoyed the pastries she made. I will always remember her face, how relaxed and calm she was when she was baking.

The recipes my mother wrote and collected during the Holocaust were very precious to her. They remained with her during the death march and throughout her journey back home to Plešivec. Years later, she took them with her from Czechoslovakia to the United States. Throughout her life when she was in a mood to bake, which was often, she looked through her recipe collection to help her decide what to make. She copied her favorite recipes into a large book. Since the women had recalled the recipes from memory, the measurements were not always accurate and she had to revise many of them.

Many years later when we were living in the United States, my mother continued baking every week. She also baked for birthdays and anniversaries and for bar-mitzvah and bat-mitzvah celebrations for each of her grandchildren. On these occasions she made all the pastries for the dessert table. She also baked for family gatherings and when entertaining. Family and friends looked forward to my mother's desserts.

Every Friday evening Shabbat was welcomed in our house, all three generations together, and we all enjoyed the challah and pastries my mother made each week. She was talented. Her breads, tortes, cookies and cakes were exceptional.

Auschwitz May 2017

My mother never went back to Auschwitz-Birkenau after the war. Both of my parents lost their families there, and it was too painful for them to go to a place where their loved ones had been brutally murdered.

My aunt Babi, however, had a strong desire to visit the Auschwitz-Birkenau concentration camp where she was once imprisoned with my mother, and in the 1970s, she returned there for a day. She was accompanied by her husband, Laci, and another couple. It turned out to be a very difficult trip for my aunt. As she stood on the premises of the former concentration camp and her memories flooded back, she fainted.

I grew up without grandparents and only knew them through the stories that my parents told me about them. It was painful for me not to have grandparents. I missed them and always felt a void in my heart. Many times I observed the special bond that my non-Jewish friends had with their grandparents, and I wished to have the same. Our family was not even able to go to the cemetery and visit their graves, because there were no graves for the victims of the Holocaust.

Since I was a child, I knew that one day I would go to Auschwitz. I always felt a need to go there and to say a prayer for my grandparents who perished there.

It took me many years until I had the courage to make such a difficult trip. I felt that I could no longer postpone it, and in May 2017, my husband, Jack, our three grown children and I embarked on this emotionally draining but very important trip.

Before going to Auschwitz, we stopped first in Košice, Slovakia, to visit my aging aunt and the rest of the family. This was the last time that I saw my aunt Babi, because she passed away a few months later.

The next day we drove to Kraków in Poland, where we stayed overnight, and the following day we went to Auschwitz. First we visited Auschwitz I and from there we went to Auschwitz II-Birkenau, which is 3 kilometers away. Birkenau was the killing center equipped with gas chambers and crematoria to which all the Hungarian Jews, including my family, were transported by train.

Almost half of the Jews killed in Auschwitz were Hungarian Jews. They were gassed within a period of about seven weeks. The mass deportations of nearly 430,000 Hungarian Jews to Auschwitz took place between May 15 and July 9, 1944. Ninety percent of the Hungarian Jews were exterminated,[63] among them my four grandparents.

It was shocking to see that vast and empty place with only few wooden

With our children (July 2018). From left: Mark, Eva, Jack, Corinne and Tommy. Photo Credit: Sofy B&B Photography.

barracks remaining, and as we followed our guide on a warm and sunny day, my mother's words immediately came to my mind. I remembered her recollection of getting off the trains and seeing a vast area without trees and grass. There was no shade to hide from the hot sun during the summer months. She often recalled the many women who got sun stroke because they stood for hours at roll calls with their bald heads under the hot sun.

Seventy-three years later, I was standing with my family in the same place, and I was in total shock. My husband, who was very tired from the trip and could not tolerate the heat of the sun, had the freedom to walk back to the main building where he could sit in the shade until he was able to join us again. This was in stark contrast to what my mother and aunt had endured.

It was very difficult for me to be there, and I knew that I could not have done this trip without the love and support of my family. We lit many candles, one for each family member who perished in the gas chambers of Birkenau. Together with my two sons and my daughter, we recited the Jewish prayer *El Maleh Rachamim* for the dead.[64] Afterward, although it was late in the afternoon, we drove all the way to Prague. I could not wait to get far away from that place where so many loved ones suffered and died.

A Legacy

We donated the artifacts we had from the Holocaust to the United States Holocaust Memorial Museum in Washington D.C. In November 2017, I personally delivered the recipes, my mother's prisoner number, her identification pin and the tie from her wooden clogs to the curator of the museum. It was difficult for me as well as for our children to part with these artifacts because they were in our family for 72 years. But we knew that it was the right decision.

I am a second-generation survivor, or what is called 2G. Am I defined by my parents' history, even though I did not live through it? Of course I am. I am affected both positively and negatively by the horrific events my parents experienced. The information about their experiences was deeply painful to me. But they were strong and resilient, and they transferred to me their resiliency and strength as well. While trauma can be transmitted across generations, so can resilience.[65] This resilience enabled me to be psychologically well adjusted and to know how to cope and adapt to challenges in my life.

We live in a world where antisemitism is on the rise, Holocaust denial and distortion of history are frequent occurrences, and there is hatred and prejudice around us.[66] Today there are very few Holocaust survivors left;[67] therefore, there is an urgency to recording and remembering survivor stories.

It is very important to remember the past and to learn from it. It is also very important that we teach the lessons of the Holocaust to younger generations. We

Our grandchildren (July 2018). Photo Credit: Sofy B&B Photography.

have the power to make better choices. It is important to treat people as equals, to show kindness and respect, and to be caring and helpful to others. We must strive to make the world a better place for everyone. The horrors of the *Shoah* must never be forgotten and must never happen again!

Initially the story of my parents was intended to be a family history book for my children and grandchildren only. But one way to prevent the Holocaust from happening again is by telling the stories. It is my duty to educate others on what happened to my family so that the six million Jews who were murdered will never be forgotten. Kindness and compassion must win over hatred.

This is the legacy I am leaving behind to my three children and six grandchildren and future generations. This is my gift to them, to share the story of my parents, grandparents and other family members, to remember them and through their story to keep their memories alive. The story of my parents and their courage continues to give me strength, and now I want to pass this strength on to my children and my children's children. It is my obligation to future generations to tell their story and to never forget.

PART THREE

The Story of Ernő

Ernő, my father, was born in 1909 into an orthodox family in Jolsva, Austria-Hungary, now Jelšava, Slovakia. The Austro-Hungarian Empire collapsed at the end of World War I, and an independent state of Czechoslovakia was founded in 1918. Jelšava became part of the newly established First Czechoslovak Republic.[68]

He was one of six children born to Etel and Jenő (Eugen) Kaufmann. His father owned a successful business of textiles, shoes and children's clothing. They had a comfortable life and they helped families who were less fortunate. Ernő attended public school in the morning and Cheder (Hebrew school) in the afternoon. After he finished four years of middle school, he joined his father to work in the family business. He studied German and was fluent in German, Hungarian, Slovak and Czech.

At the age of 21 he was drafted into the Czechoslovak army and was stationed in Prague for over a year. After returning home he continued working in the family business with his father. In 1937 he married Irénke Kesztenbaum from Beregszász (Beregovo, present-day Ukraine). After only a year of marriage, in 1938 he was drafted again to serve in the Czechoslovak army, this time near Prešov.

Ernő's hometown of Jelšava was located on the southern region of Czechoslovakia, currently Slovakia, which was annexed by Hungary in November 1938. No longer a citizen of Czechoslovakia,[69] Ernő was discharged from the Czechoslovak army and sent home. Now a citizen of Hungary, he was immediately drafted[70] by the Hungarians into their army and was sent to Miskolc, Hungary. His service in the Hungarian army lasted only a few weeks because the new anti-Jewish laws adopted by Hungary in 1938 prohibited Jews from serving in the army.

During most of World War II Hungary was allied with Germany.[71] Hungarian Jewish men were excluded from regular military service because, according to the Hungarians, Jews were "unreliable" to serve in the armed military. Instead they were recruited for mandatory *munkaszolgálat* (forced labor service) and were required to perform forced labor for the Hungarian army. They served unarmed under very harsh and often brutal conditions.

Ernő was conscripted into the Hungarian Labor Service and was taken with his unit to Tokaj, a well-known wine region. Unexpectedly, he met his father in Tokaj. Jenő was in Tokaj together with Ica's father, Károly — the two men who would become my grandfathers.

The work required at this location was digging sand out of the river with shovels. The sand was loaded onto wheelbarrows and then the heavy wheelbarrows were pushed and unloaded somewhere else. They also built bridges. The work was very strenuous for everyone but even more so for the older people. After a while my two grandfathers and the other older men were sent home.

Ernő and the rest of the younger men remained working in Tokaj until May or June 1940, and then they were also sent home. Ernő returned home and resumed work in the family business. His daughter Marika was born in 1941. He was at home for about a year and a half and was recruited for labor service once again. After this he rarely saw his wife and daughter.

On those rare occasions when Ernő was able to visit his family while he was in the forced labor unit, he never failed to visit his parents. During one of these rare visits after he had spent the night at home with his wife and daughter, he stopped by his parents' home early in the morning before returning to the forced labor unit.

His mother gave him warm soup for breakfast, because this was all she had. As he said his goodbyes to his parents, his father walked him to the door, placed his hands on top of his head and blessed him with the Hebrew Priestly Blessing.

This was the last time he saw his parents. This memory remained with him for the rest of his life. There was deep pain and sorrow in his face and tears streaming down his cheeks each time he recalled this event.

The Hungarian government passed additional anti-Jewish laws, eliminating Jews from public and cultural life, confiscating their properties and separating them from the rest of the Hungarian society. The Hungarians took away the Kaufmann family's store. Ernő's father continued to work there for a short time, but a Christian man, Mr. Kristof, was put in charge of the store. Mr. Kristof did not remain in the store for long, and he crossed the border into the Slovak region of the country to avoid being drafted. Before the war ended he returned to the Kaufmann store and became the sole worker at the store. By this time the Kaufmann family had already been deported.

Forced labor work was demanding and strenuous and the food rations were limited. Along with a small piece of bread they also received a cigarette. Ernő did not smoke and a fellow slave laborer offered his bread to him in exchange for his cigarette. Ernő gave him the cigarette and told him to keep the bread.

In 1943 Ernő was sent with a labor unit consisting of about two hundred men to work in Hejőcsaba near Miskolc, Hungary. He worked there for many months, and in the spring of 1944, he heard that his family had been taken from Jelšava to the Plešivec ghetto.

Ernő was worried that they might not be getting enough food in the ghetto and decided to send a package of food to his family. Inside the package were basic food items that he was able to obtain in the village. He sent bread, cheese, a few pieces of scallions and a few individually and carefully wrapped eggs.

After sending the first package and getting a note from his wife thanking him, he sent another package of food and again he included carefully wrapped raw eggs. Again he received a thank-you note from his wife. "Please don't send any more eggs. We get eggs in the ghetto," Irénke wrote. Ernő wondered if perhaps the eggs had arrived broken, but he never had a chance to find out.

While he was away, his wife Irénke, daughter Marika, parents Jenő and Etel, and youngest sister Vali, as well as other family members, were forced out of their homes in the spring of 1944. They were deported to Auschwitz-Birkenau. They all perished in the gas chambers with the exception of Vali, who was sent from Auschwitz to the Allendorf munitions factory in Germany and survived.

From Hungary, the forced labor unit was transferred to Poland. Ernő spent approximately seven months in Delatyn-Nadworna in Poland (present-day Ukraine). They were digging trenches all day and night near the ongoing battles between the Soviet and German armies. They wore their own clothes but were required to wear a yellow armband so they could be identified as Jews.

Toward the end of 1944, the Germans knew they were losing the war and started to escape. The Hungarian soldiers with the slave laborers began to walk toward home. They walked day and night, going through the Carpathian Mountains. They went through Beregszász, the city where Irénke came from. The men in charge of the unit stopped here to take a few hours of rest. Ernő decided to abandon his unit and escape. It was very risky and he had to be extremely cautious.

He went to the house of his in-laws, aware that his in-laws had already been deported, but hoping to hide there. When he opened the gate, he saw a Hungarian military unit all lined up and ready inside the large courtyard. Ernő soundlessly closed the gate and left.

He stopped at the neighboring house. The woman told him that he could hide upstairs in the attic, and that her husband was also there. Ernő changed his mind and left, fearing that it might be a trap.

He returned to his wife's childhood home and sneaked inside without being noticed by the military unit. A Gentile family was living in the house. While he talked to the family about the possibility of hiding there, the commander of the Hungarian army walked in, saw Ernő and inquired about him. After this he was too afraid to stay and returned to join his unit at the rest stop, careful not to be noticed.

They continued walking long distances day and night. Many men died because of the fighting around them — the war was still going on. They heard gunfire and explosions in the near distance.

Most of the forced labor units were guarded by Hungarian *Nyilas*, Arrow Cross thugs, who treated them brutally.[72] The Hungarian soldiers who were in charge of Ernő's unit were not as cruel as those in other units, but rather were indifferent toward them.

One day in November 1944, his forced labor unit stopped to spend the night in the small Slovakian village of Tupá (Hungarian: Tompa). The villagers were kind and gave them bread. A Christian man walked up to Ernő and said to him, "We have horses in the stable on the top of the mountain. Why don't you run away?" Ernő thanked him and returned to the unit.

That evening he made the decision to escape. He waited until nighttime, dozed off for a short time and then in the middle of the night, while everyone was sleeping, he got up to leave. The man who was asleep next to him woke up.

"Where are you going?" he asked.

"I am running away," Ernő replied.

"Can I come with you?" the man asked.

"Of course," Ernő said. The two men then escaped into the mountains.

They found the stable on the top of the mountain. Inside was a man with many horses. The man told them that they could not hide in the stable. He pointed to a house nearby and instructed them to go there. The people living in the house allowed them to hide in their stable. To his surprise, at least ten other men, also slave laborers, were already hiding there.

Ernő later found out that the next morning his forced labor unit was taken to the border between Hungary and Austria, and all the slave laborers were then summarily shot to death by the Hungarian soldiers.[73]

On the top of the mountain, Ernő remained hiding for eight days, always staying inside the stable. There was a second house nearby, and every day the people from both houses brought soup for all of the men who were hiding. After the eighth day, Ernő no longer heard gunfire.

Early the next morning he picked up an empty potato sack from the ground, threw it over his shoulder and went out to assess the situation. As he was going down the mountain, he ran into a small group of Russian soldiers who asked him where they could find *bor*, using the Hungarian word for wine. Ernő pointed in another direction and they left him alone. He promptly turned around and went back up to the top of the mountain to tell everyone that the Russians had arrived and that they were free. It was November 1944.

It took him two more months and a few more stops before he was able to get back home to Jelšava. The war was not yet over, and the fighting was still going on in some places. He could not continue his journey and stopped in a small village called

Riečka (Hungarian: Recske) near Banská Bystrica because he heard gunshots in the near distance. Riečka is located 109 kilometers (68 miles) west from Jelšava.

Ernő was directed toward a house and was told that other slave laborers were waiting out the war in the house. The lady of the house lived alone; she was a widow and her son was away in the war. She was very kind to the men and cooked soup for them every day. Ernő was very grateful to this older lady, and every day he went outside to chop wood for her and brought it inside the house to make fire in the stove.

The older lady* liked him very much, and a few days later when he was ready to leave, she asked him to stay, saying that she did not want him to go. Ernő explained that he could not stay — he had to go home.

Ernő continued his journey home. Once again, it was not safe to go any further and he stopped in a small village, Šivetice (Hungarian: Süvete), only 6 kilometers away from Jelšava. Many people living in this village were customers in the Kaufmann family store and knew Ernő and his parents.

He walked into the courtyard of a house and immediately a Russian soldier approached him and demanded his small rucksack. Ernő had carried it with him the entire time with a change of clean clothes and underwear. Mrs. Macko, the lady of the house who knew the Kaufmann family and was a frequent customer in their store, recognized Ernő. She quickly called out in Slovak from inside of her house, "Toto je môj syn!" ('This is my son!') The Russian soldier then backed off and left Ernő alone.

The next day was quiet and they did not hear gunshots. Ernő continued his journey walking home. He finally arrived in his hometown of Jelšava, and he walked slowly up the hill to his house. Inside his house was a Hungarian Christian family. They picked up their belongings and left.

Ernő was finally at home, in the house that he shared with his first wife and their daughter. But he was all alone. It was January 1945. He was among the first Jews to return to Jelšava. The war was not yet over, but he was able to remain in his house until the war ended.

---

* A few years after the war the older lady found out that Ernő got married. She traveled to Plešivec to visit Ernő and also meet Ica. She and Ernő hugged each other. She told him how much she loved him and that during the war she wanted to adopt him for a son.

Kaufmann Family

argo, Ernő's sister, lived in Košice after getting married in 1930s and later moved to Prešov. She was in hiding during the war with her husband, Ignác (Irving), and their nine-year-old daughter, Vierka. Margo and her family survived the war with the help of Mr. Václav Čermák, a Baptist pastor, who hid and protected the family during the war. Mr. Čermák is honored in the Yad Vashem Holocaust Museum in Jerusalem and his name is listed as the Righteous Among the Nations, commemorating his courage and compassion.[74] Margo and Irving had a second child, a son named Joe, who was born after the war. They immigrated to the United States.

Ernő's sister Klári, and her husband, Adolf, lived in Sečovce, Slovakia, and they made a decision to go into hiding without their children. They sent their daughter, who was also named Vierka, and son, Adi (a diminutive of Adam), to Jelšava, which during the war was part of Hungary, assuming that they would be safer in Hungary with Klári's parents. While they were in hiding, their two young children were deported with their grandparents and perished in the gas chambers. Klári and Adolf survived. They had a son, Ivan, who was born after the war. The three of them immigrated to Israel and later to the United States.

Ernő's sister Vali was deported with his parents, his wife and child, his sister Klári's two children and his brother Sanyi's wife and two sons. Out of the ten members of the Kaufmann family who had been deported to Auschwitz-Birkenau, Vali was the sole survivor. She got married after the war and lived in Putnok, Hungary, and then later in Budapest with her husband, Lajos, and daughter, Livia, until 1963, when they also immigrated to the United States.

Ernő's youngest brother, Dönci (Ödön or Edmund), was 22 years old in early 1942. He had completed business school and was drafted into the Hungarian Forced Labor Service. Thousands of young Jewish men were sent by train as forced laborers with the Hungarian Second Army to the Eastern Russian Front, Dönci among them.

The train went through Plešivec where it stopped for a day to gather others from nearby regions. Dönci's father asked him to visit the Kellner family. Ica remembered that he stopped by with a friend and they were invited to stay for lunch. When it was time for them to leave, Ica and her father walked them back to the train station. The train was full of young Jewish men. These young men were taken directly to the Russian front. A fierce fight took place at the bend of the River Don between the Soviet Red Army and the German and Hungarian armies. They were near Stalingrad where the biggest battle was fought. The Battle of Stalingrad was one of the worst in history with more casualties than any battle before.[75]

Ernő remembered that his parents received a few letters from Dönci, but then the letters stopped coming. The young Jewish slave laborers were unarmed, inadequately clothed during the extremely harsh winter and subjected to cruel harassment by the Hungarian officers and soldiers who were in charge of them. They were ordered by the Hungarian army to clear the minefields with their bare hands, even while the battle was raging, and were caught in the crossfire. Over forty thousand young Jewish forced laborers perished there, including Dönci.

Ernő never found out the cause of his brother's death. Was he cruelly treated by the Hungarian officers and soldiers in charge? Did he starve or freeze to death? Was he overcome by a disease or blown up while picking up field mines?

Ernő's oldest brother, Sanyi (Alexander), was in a forced labor unit that was immediately taken to Russia near Minsk, today the capital of Belarus. The man in charge of his unit selected 40 men to pick mines, and Sanyi was among them. Then he looked them over one more time and pointed at Sanyi. "Take that small man back and take this taller one instead," he said. The taller man looked at Sanyi with sad eyes. "Now I will die in your place," he told him. Sanyi was sent back home to his family.

He did not stay at home long and soon he was summoned for slave labor once again. Sanyi and the rest of the men in this small unit were very fortunate. The Hungarian Army Officer who was the commander of the unit, Lieutenant Imrich Lackner, was from Jelšava.[76] He had a few good friends among these men — one of them was Sanyi.

When Mr. Lackner received an order to take his unit to the front where fierce fighting was going on, he disobeyed his orders. "Come with me, listen to me and don't talk about it. We will go this way," he told his men. Mr. Lackner took his men in a different direction and, in doing so, saved the lives of about 25 Jewish men. His own life was in danger because of what he had done, but he was a decent man and never regretted his decision.

A few years after the war, the men he saved wrote a letter to the Yad Vashem Holocaust Museum in Jerusalem. The letter was signed by many of the men, including Sanyi. Mr. Lackner was honored by Israel as a Righteous Among the Nations, an award given to non-Jews who risked their lives to rescue Jews during World War II.

At the end of the war, Sanyi also returned to an empty house. His wife, Elza, and two young sons, Robi and Tomi, had been deported with the rest of Ernő's family and perished in Auschwitz-Birkenau. Sanyi remarried and with his second wife, Lili, had a daughter, Esther. After the war they immigrated to Israel.

After the loss of his wife and daughter, Ernő was left all alone. Then one day Ica walked into his store. After he met her, he knew that he wanted to marry her and start a new life with her. They got married within a few months.

FAMILY PHOTOS

Front row left to right: My maternal grandfather, Károly (Karl) Kellner, Babi, my maternal grandmother, Jolán Kellner, and Ica. Back row left to right: My mother's cousins Ella Grünmann and Vera Foltýn (ca. 1932). From Moreimi family archives.

My paternal grandparents, Jenő (Eugen) and Etel Kaufmann. From Moreimi family archives.

Ernő's first daughter, Marika Kaufmann (ca. 1941). From Moreimi family archives.

Vierka and Adi Birnbaum (my aunt Klári and uncle Adolf's children). From Moreimi family archives.

Dönci (Ödön/Edmund) Kaufmann, Ernő's youngest brother. From Moreimi family archives.

My father's brother Sanyi (Alexander) Kaufmann with his first family: wife, Elza, and sons, Tomi and Robi. From Moreimi family archives.

Ernő with his sisters. From left: Klári, Vali and Margo (1994). From Moreimi family archives.

Our family (July 2018). From left: Jody, Tommy, Eva, Jack, Jen, Mark, Corinne and our six grandchildren.
Photo Credit: Sofy B&B Photography.

RECIPES

The following recipes were shared with my mother by her fellow inmates in the subcamp of Buchenwald. The recipes were given from memory and were not always accurate. Therefore, my mother had to revise many of them. Following are a few of the recipes my mother revised.

Linzer Cookies

Approximately 36 cookies

The Linzer and Ischler (next page) cookies date back to the Austro-Hungarian Empire and even today they remain very popular in both Austria and Hungary. Linzer cookies are based on the Linzer torte, named after the Austrian town Linz.

    Linzer and Ischler cookies are very similar. Both are preserve-filled round cookie sandwiches. Linzer cookies have a small hole cut in the center of the top cookie, while the top of the Ischler cookie is covered with chocolate glaze.

Ingredients

14 oz/400 g unbleached all-
  purpose flour
¼ tsp baking soda
4 oz/130 g granulated sugar
½ cup finely ground walnuts
2 egg yolks
8 oz/226 g (2 sticks) sweet
  unsalted butter,
  softened (not melted)
¼ cup milk
Jam for in-between the 2
  cookies — I prefer
  a tart jam like a seedless
  red currant or raspberry
  jelly, but apricot jam
  (smooth, without
  pieces of fruit) can
  also be used.
Powdered sugar, for garnish

Instructions

Preheat oven to 350°F. Line 2 baking sheets with parchment paper.

1. In a bowl, mix the flour and baking soda and then add the sugar, walnuts, egg yolks, butter and milk.

2. Knead with your hands until the dough is smooth. Refrigerate for one hour.

3. Roll out the dough on a lightly floured surface to a thickness of about 0.5 cm, or slightly less than ¼ inch.

4. With a round cookie cutter that is 2 to 2½ inches in diameter, cut out the cookies. Gather the scrap dough, knead, roll out and repeat.
   There should be a total of approximately 72 pieces

5. For one-half of the cookies, use a ½-inch diameter cookie cutter to cut out the center. These will be the top halves of the cookies.

6. Bake for 15–20 minutes or until light brown.

To assemble: When the cookies are cool, stir the jam to loosen and then spread the jam on each solid round cookie. Top the jam-covered cookie with a cookie with a cut-out center. Cookies can be stored in an airtight container for a few days, or they can be frozen. Dust with powdered sugar before serving.

Ischler Cookies

Approximately 36 cookies

The Ischler cookies were made especially for Emperor Franz Joseph and became his favorite. They were named after the Austrian town Bad Ischl, where the emperor established his summer residence.

Ingredients

14 oz/400 g unbleached
      all-purpose flour
¼ tsp baking soda
4 oz/130 g granulated sugar
½ cup finely ground walnuts
2 egg yolks
8 oz/226 g (2 sticks) sweet
      unsalted butter,
      softened (not melted)
¼ cup milk
Jam for in-between the 2
      cookies — I prefer
      a tart jam like
      a seedless red currant
      or raspberry jelly, but
      apricot jam (smooth,
      without pieces of fruit)
      can also be used.

Chocolate glaze:

3 T Hershey's unsweetened
      cocoa powder
3 T sugar
3 T water
1 oz/30 g sweet unsalted
      butter

Instructions

Preheat oven to 350°F. Prepare 2 cookie sheets lined with parchment paper.

1. In a bowl, mix the flour and baking soda and then add sugar, walnuts, egg yolks, butter and milk.
2. Knead with your hands until the dough is smooth. Refrigerate for one hour.
3. Roll out the dough on a lightly floured surface to a thickness of about 0.5 cm, or slightly less than ¼ inch.
4. With a round cookie cutter that is 2 to 2½ inches in diameter, cut out the cookies. Gather the scrap dough, knead, roll out and repeat. There should be a total of approximately 72 pieces.
5. Bake for 15–20 minutes or until light brown.

To assemble: When the cookies are cool, spread jam on top of a cookie and then cover it with another cookie. When all done, begin preparing the chocolate glaze.

Chocolate glaze:

1. In a small pan mix the cocoa powder, sugar and water. Cook on a low to medium heat stirring until the glaze thickens.
2. Remove from heat and add the butter. Mix well.
3. Spread warm chocolate glaze on top of each cookie. Allow glaze to set. Cookies can be stored in an airtight container, with each layer separated by wax paper, and refrigerated for a few days, or they can be frozen.

Sour Cherry Cake

Ingredients

6 eggs, separated

8 oz sweet unsalted butter
or margarine,
softened (not
melted), plus a little
extra for the baking
sheet

7 oz/200 g sugar

Vanilla extract

½ tsp baking powder

10 oz/300 g unbleached all-
purpose flour

Sour cherries — I use pitted
sour cherries, they are
in a light syrup in a
glass jar. Instead
of the sour cherries
you can use fresh
sweet cherries
halved, raspberries or
sliced strawberries.

Powdered sugar, for garnish

Instructions

Preheat oven to 350°F. Prepare a 13 x 9 x 2 inch buttered and floured baking sheet.

1. Beat the egg whites until stiff, and set aside.
2. In a separate bowl beat together butter, sugar and vanilla until pale and fluffy. Add the egg yolks and beat until well blended.
3. Mix the baking powder into the flour and add the flour to the mixture. Mix only until incorporated — do not overmix.
4. With a wooden spoon, gently fold in the stiffly beaten egg whites.
5. Pour the batter into the buttered and floured baking sheet and bake for 10 minutes.
6. Remove from oven and sprinkle the pitted cherries on top of the batter. Continue baking for a total of 40–50 minutes until golden brown.
7. Let cool and cut into squares about 2 x 2 inches. Dust the top with powdered sugar before serving.

Gerbeaud Slices

Zserbó szelet is among one of the best-known Hungarian desserts. It was invented by Emil Gerbeaud, a French, Swiss-born *pâtissier* who moved to Budapest in the 1800s to take charge of a patisserie owned by Henrik Kugler. When Kugler retired, he sold the patisserie to Gerbeaud, who remodeled the space into a posh dining experience. Many famous people visited the elegant café, including the Habsburg royal family. Even today *Gerbeaud Cukrászda* remains one of the most elegant cafés in Europe. The café serves a wide variety of wonderful pastries, among them one of their signature desserts — Gerbeaud slices.

Ingredients

Dough

Proofing yeast

1 envelope active dry yeast

¼ cup warm milk (110°F)

1 tsp flour

½ tsp sugar

17.6 oz/500 g unbleached all-
    purpose flour

½ tsp baking powder

8.8 oz/250 g sweet unsalted
    butter (2 sticks),
    cubed, at room
    temperature

1 egg

2 yolks

1½ T sugar

Filling

9 oz/250 g ground walnuts

7 oz/200 g granulated sugar

½ tsp cinnamon

Jam

Chocolate glaze

3 T Hershey's unsweetened
    cocoa powder

3 T sugar

3 T water

1 oz/30 g sweet unsalted butter

Instructions

Preheat oven to 350°F. Prepare a 16 x 10 x 1½ or 15 x 9 x 1½ inch buttered and floured baking sheet.

1. Dissolve yeast in warm milk. Add 1 tsp flour and ½ tsp sugar. Cover and let rise for 5–10 minutes in a warm place.

2. In a large bowl mix 17.6 oz/500 g flour and baking powder and then add the cubed butter.

3. Add the egg, yolks, 1½ T sugar and yeast mixture. Mix well and knead to form a dough. Add more flour if necessary, or a few drops of milk if dry.

4. Divide dough into 3 equal portions. On a floured surface, roll each portion one at a time to match the size of the baking sheet.

5. In a separate bowl, combine the walnuts, 7 oz/200 g sugar and cinnamon. Set aside.

6. Place the first portion of dough on a floured baking sheet, pressing it into the corners. Spread jam on top and sprinkle half of the walnut mixture evenly over the entire surface.

7. Cover with the second portion of dough. Spread jam on top and add the remaining walnut mixture.

8. Cover with the third portion of dough and gently press down with your fingers.

9. Bake for approximately 40–45 minutes or until medium brown.

10. Let cool completely.

11. In a small pan, mix the cocoa powder, sugar and water, and cook on a low to medium heat stirring often. When slightly thickened, remove from heat and add the butter. Mix well and while still warm spread on top of the cake.

12. When the chocolate glaze is dry, cut into slices 2 inches long and ½ inch wide. Use a sharp knife dipped in hot water.

Chocolate Almond Torte

Approximately 12-15 servings

This torte can be made in a rectangular baking sheet or in two round cake forms. My mother made it for many occasions, including birthdays or anniversary celebrations. Hazelnuts or walnuts can be used instead of almonds.

Ingredients

Cake

7 eggs, separated
7 heaping T of granulated sugar
2 oz bittersweet chocolate,
    softened
½ tsp baking powder
7 flat T unbleached all-purpose
    flour

Filling/Crème

5 oz/140 g sweet unsalted butter,
    softened at room
    temperature
5 oz/140 g sugar
5 oz/140 g ground almonds
3–4 T milk
1 tsp vanilla essence

Instructions

Preheat oven to 350°F. Prepare a buttered and floured baking sheet either approximately 13 x 9 x 2 inches or two 9-inch-diameter round cake forms.

1. Beat the 7 egg whites until stiff, and put aside.
2. In a separate bowl beat the egg yolks and sugar until pale and creamy.
3. Add the softened chocolate and mix well.
4. Mix the baking powder into the flour and add to the egg yolk, sugar and chocolate mixture at a low speed.
5. Gently fold in the egg whites, but do not mix.
6. Bake about 36–40 minutes in the rectangle baking pan or approximately 25–30 minutes in the two round cake forms, until a toothpick inserted in the center comes out clean.
7. Let cool.

Crème preparation for filling:

1. In a bowl mix the butter and sugar, and set it aside.
2. In a saucepan cook the ground almonds with the milk for about 3 minutes on a low to medium heat, mixing constantly.
3. When the almonds are softened, remove from heat, add vanilla essence and mix in the butter and sugar mixture.
4. Refrigerate for 30–60 minutes until it is spreadable.

To assemble: If a rectangular baking sheet was used, then cut the cake lengthwise into half. Spread a thin layer of crème on the top half of the cake and the remainder in the middle of the cake. If using two round cake forms, place them on top of each other with crème in between and on the top. Refrigerate or freeze until ready to serve.

Wasp Nest (*Darázsfészek*)

This yeast dough is made with walnuts, but it can also be made without nuts. Simply omit the walnuts and add vanilla essence to the butter and sugar mixture and spread it on the rolled-out dough. In Europe the *Darázsfészek* was served for lunch, but it can also be served as a dessert.

Ingredients

Proofing yeast
1 envelope dry yeast
¾ cup lukewarm milk
1 tsp flour
½ tsp sugar

Dough
3½ cup unbleached
        all-purpose flour
3 egg yolks
1 tsp vanilla essence
¾ cup lukewarm milk

Filling
6 oz sweet unsalted butter
        (1½ sticks), softened at
        room temperature
¾ cup granulated sugar
½ tsp cinnamon
3 cup/12 oz ground walnuts

Instructions

Prepare a 9-inch round Bundt cake pan, generously buttered. Use about 2 tablespoons for buttering the cake pan and the remainder of the butter for the dough.

1. Dissolve the yeast in ¾ cup lukewarm milk and add 1 tsp flour and ½ tsp sugar. Cover and let it rise for 5–10 minutes.

2. In a large bowl mix the flour, egg yolks, vanilla, ¾ cup lukewarm milk and yeast mixture. You should have a very soft, light dough. Cover and let it rise for 30–45 minutes.

3. Roll out the dough on a floured surface until thin. Mix the softened butter and sugar together, and spread it over the entire surface of the dough.

4. Mix together the cinnamon and walnuts, and sprinkle over the top of the buttered dough.

5. Carefully roll the dough as a jelly roll. Cut into 1½ inch slices. Close one side by gently pinching and place into the cake pan, with the open side up. Continue and place slices next to each other, and if necessary, start a second layer on top of the first. Cover and let rise for about 1½ hours or until doubled in size.

6. Bake in a preheated 350°F oven until medium brown, approximately 50–55 minutes. Remove from oven and turn upside down on a round plate. To serve, cut and break apart while still warm.

WWII PAPERS

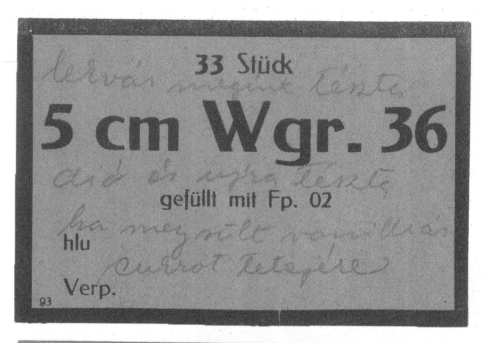

Kugel with Rolls Dipped in Wine. By Vali.

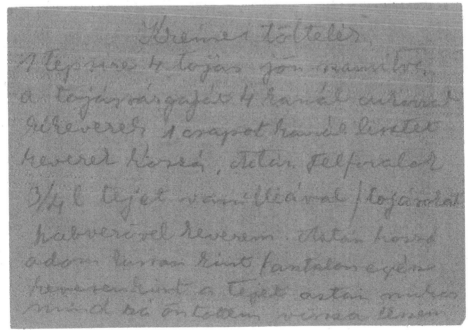

Vanilla Custard Filling for Napoleons. By Mrs. Gersch (Wife of Dr. Gersch).

Calf Liver Croquette. By Lulu.

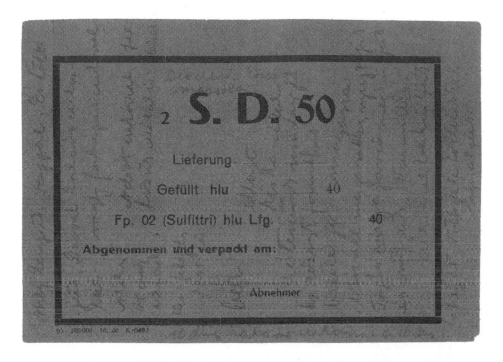

Wasp Nest. By Piri.

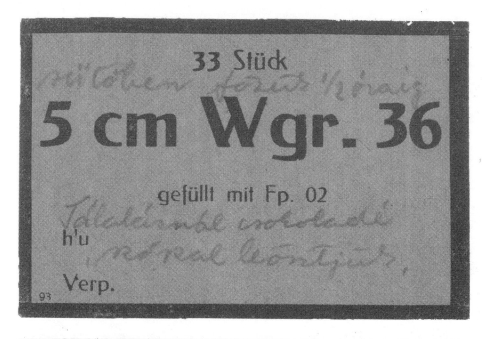

Almond Pudding. By Pani.

Hessisch-Lichtenau, den............

Zutritt -Schein
=====================

Herr...

ist berechtigt, Gebäude.................................

an folgenden Tagen ....

von:.........Uhr bis .:......Uhr zu betreten.

....

Datum..........   Betrieb

Chestnut Roll. By Irén néni.

Chocolate Bomb. By Magda Fischer.

Hessisch-Lichtenau, den............

Zutritt -Schein
==========================

Herr...

ist berechtigt, Gebäude...............................
an folgenden Tagen ....
von:.........Uhr bis ....Uhr zu betreten.

....

Datum............   Betrieb

Gerbeaud Slices. By Mariska.

33 Stück

5 cm Wgr. 36

gefüllt mit Fp. 02

hlu

Verp.

93

Deep Fried Potato and Cabbage Dough. By Mrs. Demeter.

Sugar Pretzel. By Rózsi Kopp.

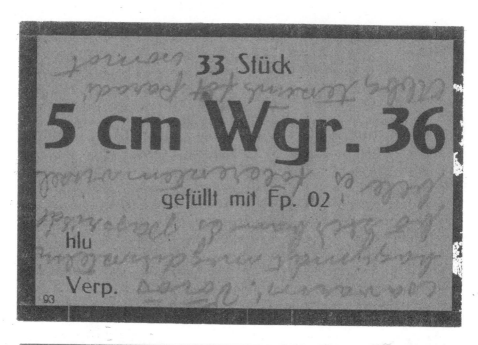

Meat Roulade. By Ilus néni.

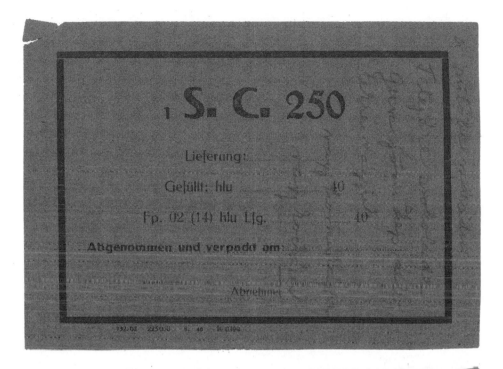

Fig Pastries. By Mariska.

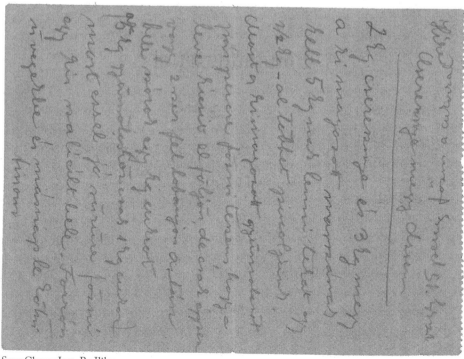

Empfangszettel

Gebäude Nr. .... Schicht: ....

Name: .... Nr. ....

Gegenstand: ....

....

Alter Gegenstand eingetauscht? Ja — nein

Datum: .... Meister: ....

169/109 100—100 4. 44 K/0499

Sour Cherry Jam. By Ilike.

Cabbage with Sour cream. By Piri.

Magdalene Cookies. By Etel Jámbor, wife of Dr. Jámbor from Zalaegerszeg.

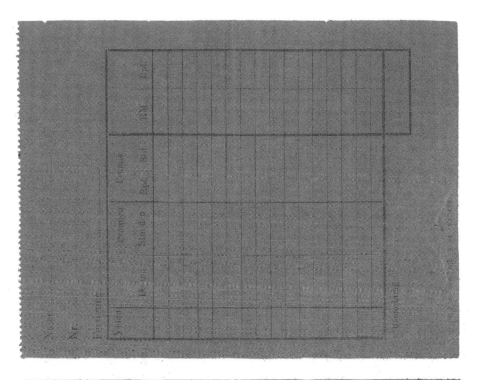

Purple Turkish Pepper Spread. By Rózsi.

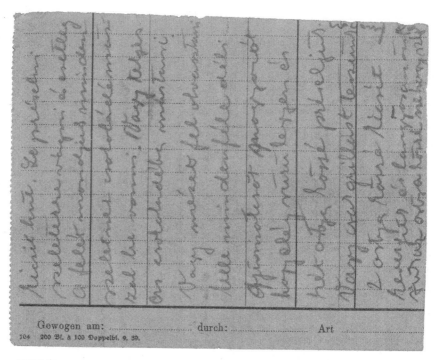

Gewogen am: .... durch: .... Art ....

704   200 Bl. à 100 Doppelbl. 9, 39.

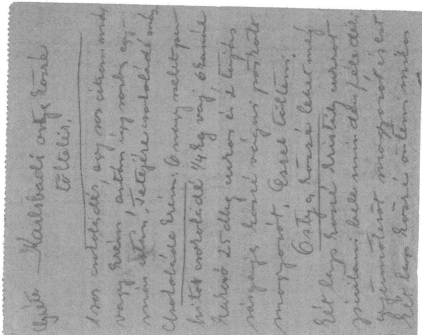

Crème Filling for Carlsbad Wafers. By Gréte.

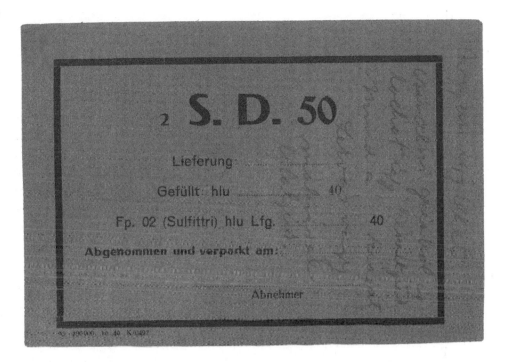

Rice Cake. By Ida.

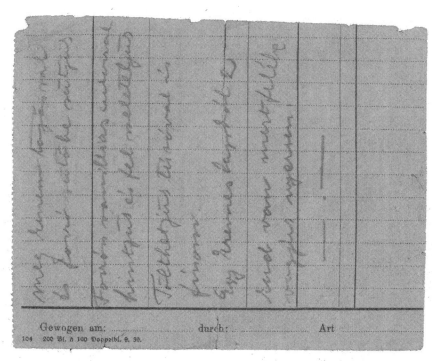

Delicious Buttery Poppy Seed and Walnut Cake. By Rózsi Breitbart.

Empfangszettel

Gebäude Nr. .... Schicht: ....

Name: .... Nr. ....

Gegenstand: ....

....

Alter Gegenstand eingetauscht?   Ja — nein

Datum: .... Meister: ....

169/169   169–100   11. 43   K/0492

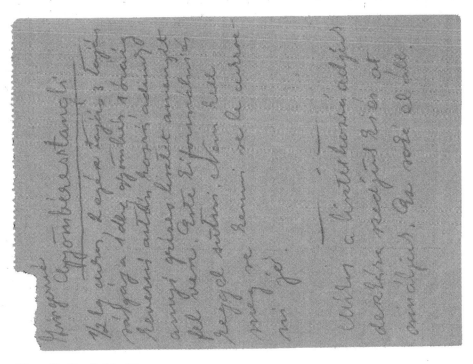

Ginger Cookies. By Mrs. Zinger.

Farmer Cheese Dumplings. By Mariska.

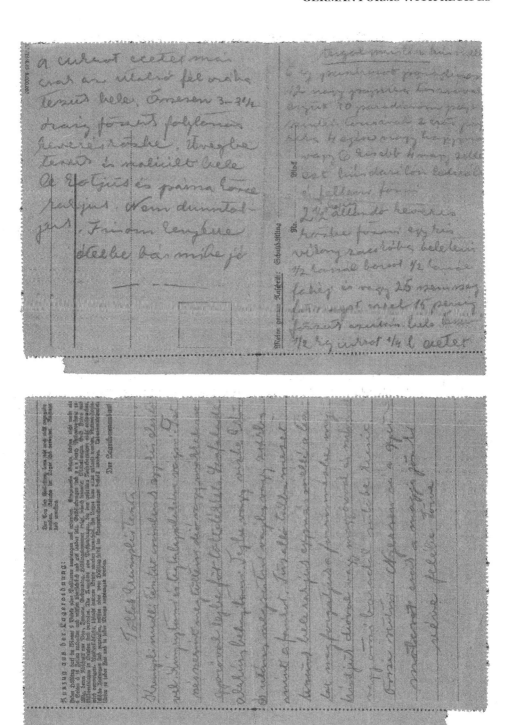

Potato Noodles Stuffed / English Mustard Sauce to go with Meat.

Schicht:				Gebäude:
Tri-Bestand				
	Bestand bei Schichtbeginn	Zugang	Abgang	Bestand bei Schichtschluß
Kessel				
Kessel				
Kessel				
Kessel				

den _____

540 100 St. à 100 F. 41   5/ 04. 9

Schichtmeister

Ischler Cookies. By Mariska.

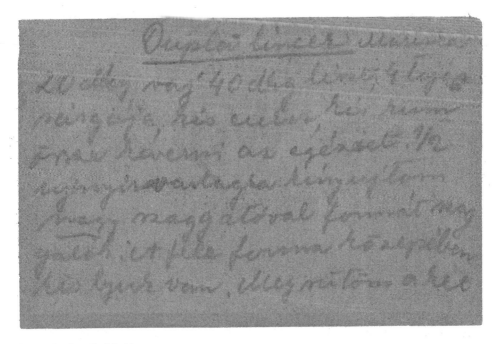

Linzer Cookies. By Mariska.

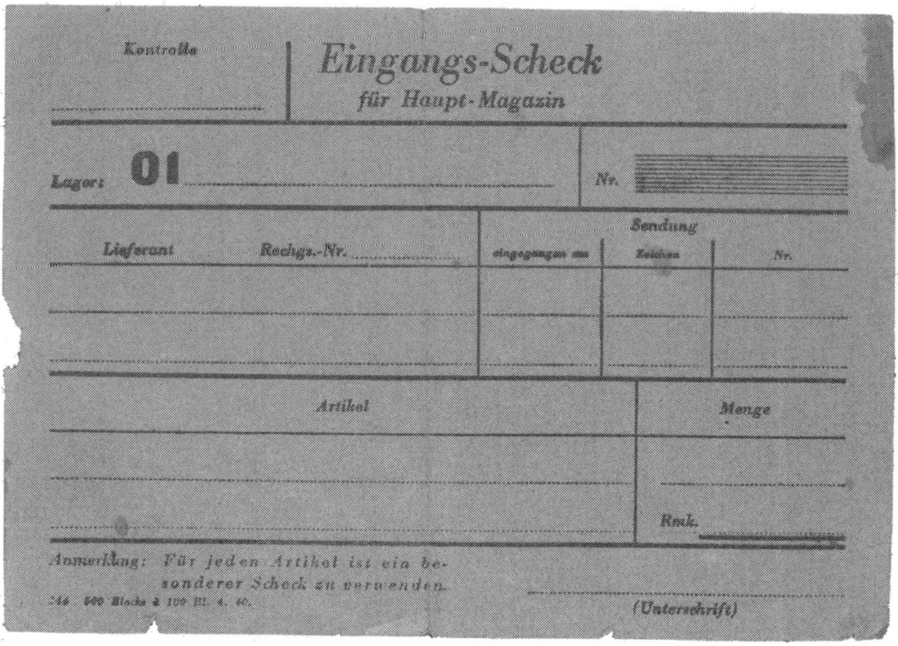

Kontrolle

Eingangs-Scheck
für Haupt-Magazin

Lager: **01**   Nr.

Lieferant	Rechgs.-Nr.	eingegangen am	Zeichen	Nr.

Sendung

Artikel	Menge

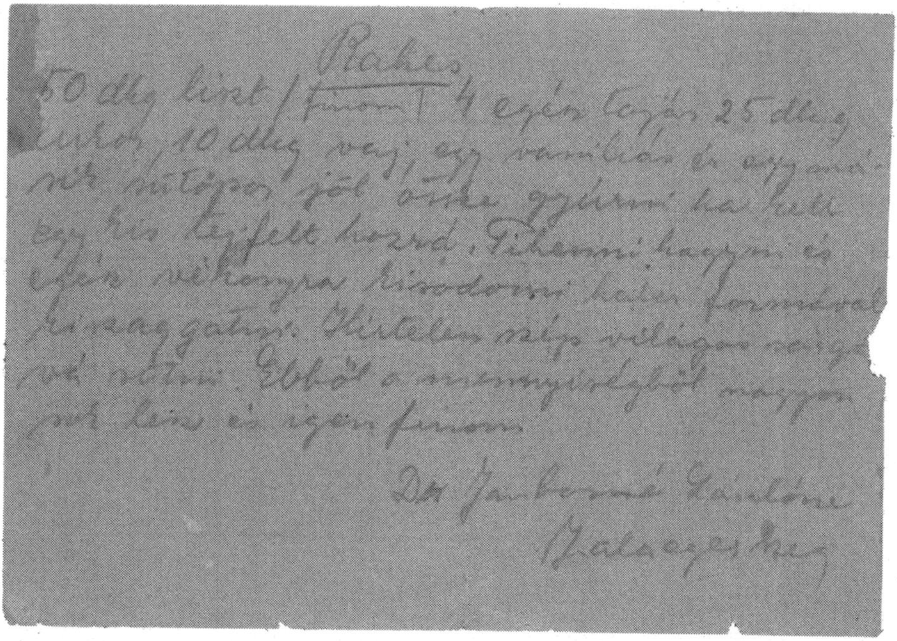

Rmk.

Anmerkung: Für jeden Artikel ist ein besonderer Scheck zu verwenden.
246 500 Blocke à 100 Bl. 4. 60.

(Unterschrift)

Rahes. By Mrs. Jámbor (Wife of Dr. Lászlo Jámbor) from Zalaegerszeg.

156

Empfangszettel

Gebäude Nr. .... Schicht: ....

Name: .... Nr. ....

Gegenstand: ....

....

Alter Gegenstand eingetauscht? Ja — nein

Datum: .... Meister: ....

100/102   100—100   11. 43   K/0499

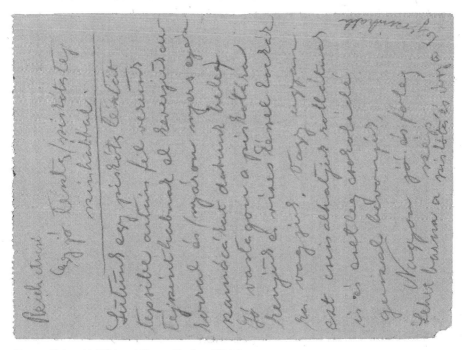

Sponge Cake with Whipped Cream. By Ancsi Reich.

Endnotes

1. Conference on Jewish Material Claims Against Germany. "New Survey by Claims Conference Finds Significant Lack of Holocaust Knowledge in the United States." http://www.claimscon.org/study/. Accessed August 17, 2019.

2. Terese Pencak Schwartz. "Non-Jewish Victims of the Holocaust." Jewishvirtuallibrary.org. https://www.jewishvirtuallibrary.org/non-jewish-victims-of-the-holocaust.

3. Meyer JV, Meyer AD. *June Meyer's Authentic Hungarian Heirloom Recipes.* United States: Meyer & Associates; 2012.

4. Storm J, Storm K. Prague, Vienna, Budapest, Beyond: An Epic Central Europe Itinerary. Our Escape Clause. https://www.ourescapeclause.com/prague-vienna-budapest-central-europe-itinerary/. Published July 12, 2019. Accessed August 17, 2019.

5. Wolfgang Benz, et al. *Der Ort Des Terrors: Geschichte Der Nationalsozialistischen Konzentrationslager / 1 Die Organisation Des Terrors.* München: Beck; 2006.

6. Wilkinson J, Hughes H. *Contemporary Europe: A History.* Prentice Hall; 2009.

7. PETROF, spol. s r.o. History | PETROF, spol. s r.o. Petrof.com. https://www.petrof.com/history. Published 2009. Accessed August 17, 2019.

8. Bergan R. Marta Eggerth obituary. the Guardian. https://www.theguardian.com/film/2013/dec/30/marta-eggerth. Published November 30, 2017.

Accessed August 17, 2019.

9. Glassheim E. National Mythologies and Ethnic Cleansing: The Expulsion of Czechoslovak Germans in 1945. *Central European History.* 2000;33(4):463-486. doi:10.1163/156916100746428.

10. Tucker SC. *Encyclopedia of World War II: A Political, Social, and Military History.* Santa Barbara: ABC-CLIO; 2005.

11. Aronson S. *Hitler, the Allies, and the Jews.* Cambridge: Cambridge Univ. Press; 2006.

12. Laqueur W, Baumel-Schwartz J, Rothkirchen L. *Slovakia. The Holocaust Encyclopedia.* New Haven: Yale University Press; 2001:595-600.

13. Axworthy M. *Axis Slovakia: Hitler's Slavic Wedge, 1938-1945.* Bayside, NY: Axis Europa Books; 2002.

14. Deák L. *Viedenská Arbitráž.* 1,2. Martin: Matica Slovenská; 1991.

15. Holocaust Educational Resource. Nizkor.org. http://www.nizkor.org/ftp.cgi/ imt/nca/nca-01/nca-01-13-spoliation-02. Published 2012. Accessed August 17, 2019.

16. Burachovič S. History of Karlovy Vary. Kr-karlovarsky.cz. http://cestovani.kr-karlovarsky.cz/en/pronavstevniky/Turistickecile/JN/Pages/KarlovyVary aspx. Published 2019. Accessed August 17, 2019.

17. Jewish Telegraphic Agency. "Nuremberg Laws Proclaimed in Czech Protectorate by President Hacha", March 24, 1942.

18. Israel Y. *Rescuing the Rebbe of Belz: Belzer Chassidus: History, Rescue and Rebirth.* Brooklyn, NY: Mesorah Publications; 2005.

19. Askey N. *Operation Barbarossa: The Complete Organisational and Statistical Analysis, and Military Simulation.* U.S.: Ingramsparks Publishing; 2014.

20. Stangneth B, Martin R. *Eichmann before Jerusalem: The Unexamined Life of a Mass Murderer.* London: Vintage Books; 2016.

21. Egressy G. A Statistical Overview of the Hungarian Numerus Clausus Law of 1920: A Historical Necessity or the First Step toward the Holocaust? *East European Quarterly.* 2000;34(4):447. https://www.questia.com/read/1G1-69372508/a-statistical-overview-of-the-hungarian-numerus-clausus. Accessed August 17, 2019.

22. Patai R. *The Jews of Hungary: History, Culture, Psychology.* Detroit, MI: Wayne State Univ. Press; 1999.

23. Reeves T. *Shoes along the Danube: Based on a True Story.* Durham, CT: Strategic Book Group; 2011.

24. Fleming M. Allied Knowledge of Auschwitz: A (Further) Challenge to the "Elusiveness" Narrative. *Holocaust and Genocide Studies.* 2014;28(1):31-57. doi:10.1093/hgs/dcu014.

25. Jewish Telegraphic Agency. Hungarian Jews residing in small towns to be deported to Ghettos in large cities: May 1, 1944.

26. Rees L. *Auschwitz: A New History.* New York, NY: Public Affairs; 2005.

27. Gutman I, Berenbaum M, United States Holocaust Memorial Museum. *Anatomy of the Auschwitz Death Camp.* Washington, DC: Indiana University Press; 1998.

28. Rees L. The Life of an Auschwitz Guard. POLITICO. https://www.politico.eu/article/auschwitz-guard-germany-holocaust-history-world-war/. Published July 15, 2015.

29. Kádár G, Vági Z, Egyesület H. *Hullarablás: A Magyar Zsidók Gazdasági Megsemmisítése.* Budapest: Jaffa; 2005.

30. Kraus O, Kulka E. *Halálgyár.* Budapest: Kossuth K; 1958.

31. Strzelecki A. *Der Raub Des Besitzes Der Opfer Des KL Auschwitz.* Hefte von Aushwitz. 21:7-99.

32. Auschwitz. Ushmm.org. https://encyclopedia.ushmm.org/content/en/article auschwitz. Published 2013.

33. Kádár G, Vági Z. Magyarok Auschwitzban. In: *Holocaust Füzetek 12.* Budapest: Magyar Auschwitz Alapítvány-Holocaust Dokumentációs Központ; 1999:92-123.

34. Debórah Dwork and Robert Jan van Pelt, *Auschwitz.* New York: Norton, 2002.

35. Mandelbaum H, Bartosik I, Willma A, Brand WR. *I Was at the Auschwitz Crematorium: A Conversation with Henryk Mandelbaum, Former Prisoner and Member of the Sonderkommando at Auschwitz.* Oświęcim, Poland: Auschwitz-Birkenau State Museum; 2011.

36. Müller F, Freitag H, Flatauer S, Bauer Y. *Eyewitness Auschwitz: Three Years in*

the Gas Chambers. Chicago: Ivan R. Dee; 1999.

37. Zimmerman J. Body Disposal at Auschwitz: The End of Holocaust-Denial. Phdn.org.https://phdn.org/archives/holocaust-history.org/auschwitz/body-disposal/. Published October 15, 1999. Accessed August 17, 2019.

38. South African Air Force. Birkenau Extermination Complex, Oswiecim, Poland; 1944. Yadvashem.org. https://www.yadvashem.org/yv/en/exhibitions/through-the-lens/images/auschwitz-aerial-photos/01.jpg. Accessed August 17, 2019.

39. Jewish Telegraphic Agency. Witness Testifies on Gestapo Forcing Jews to Misguide Relatives: May 28, 1964.

40. "Waldsee 1944," shown in Berlin, Ulm, and New York City (May 1, 2005 - December 31, 2005). http://almaondobbin.org/exhibition/waldsee-1944-1

41. Ghermezian S. Woman Who Survived Auschwitz Concentration Camp Because Nazis Ran Out of Gas Turns 101. Algemeiner.com. https://www.algemeiner.com/2014/12/11/woman-who-survived-auschwitz-concentration-camp-because-nazis-ran-out-of-gas-turns-101/. Published 2014. Accessed August 17, 2019.

42. Ferencz BB. *Less than Slaves: Jewish Forced Labor and the Quest for Compensation.* Bloomington, ID: Indiana University Press; 2002.

43. Vaupel D. *Das Außenkommando Hessisch Lichtenau Des Konzentrationslagers Buchenwald 1944/45: E. Dokumentation.* Kassel: Verl. Gesamthochschulbibliothek; 1984.

44. Auschwitz to Hessisch Lichtenau Transport List. Jewishgen.org. https://www.jewishgen.org/databases/Holocaust/0210_Hessich_Lichtenau.html. Published 2010. Accessed August 17, 2019.

45. Isaacson JM. *Seed of Sarah: Memoirs of a Survivor.* Urbana, IL: University of Illinois Press; 1991.

46. Braham RL, City University of New York; Institute for Holocaust Studies. *Studies on the Holocaust in Hungary.* Canberra: Department of Defence; 2002.

47. United States Holocaust Memorial Museum. Circular metal pin owned by a female Hungarian Jewish slave laborer - Collections Search.

Ushmm.org. https://collections.ushmm.org/search/catalog/irn594873. Published 2017. Accessed August 17, 2019.

48. Dobos E, Horváth Z. Gerbeaud Cafe Budapest Vörösmarty Square. Budapestbylocals.com. https://www.budapestbylocals.com/gerbeaud-cafe html. Published 2014. Accessed August 17, 2019.

49. Mais Y, Museum of Jewish Heritage - A Living Memorial to the Holocaust. *Daring to Resist: Jewish Defiance in the Holocaust.* New York, NY; 2007.

50. Rabbi Scherman N. and Rabbi Zlotowitz M. "*Renov Edition: Shabbat and Festival Siddur*" ArtScroll/Mesorah Publications; 1998.

51. Potemkin A, Special to RBTH. Elbe Day: A handshake that made history. Rbth.com. https://www.rbth.com/arts/2015/04/25/elbe_day_a_ handshake_that_made_history_45455.html. Published April 25, 2015. Accessed August 18, 2019.

52. Anesi C. United States Strategic Bombing Survey: Summary Report (European War). Anesi.com. https://www.anesi.com/ussbs02.htm. Published 2018. Accessed August 18, 2019.

53. Abrams BF. The End of Czechoslovak Democracy and the Rise of Communism in Eastern Europe. In: *The Struggle for the Soul of the Nation: Czech Culture and the Rise of Communism.* Lanham, MD: Rowman & Littlefield; 2005:275-288.

54. Rick Rodgers, *Kaffeehaus: Exquisite Desserts from the Cafes of Vienna, Budapest, and Prague.* New York: Clarkson Potter, 2002.

55. Grünberg K. Contaminated Generativity: Holocaust Survivors and Their Children in Germany. *The American Journal of Psychoanalysis.* 2007;67(1):82-96. doi:10.1057/palgrave.ajp.3350005.

56. Milestones: 1961–1968 - Office of the Historian. State.gov. https://history. state.gov/milestones/1961-1968/soviet-invasion-czechoslavkia. Accessed August 18, 2019.

57. Masari J. Psychiatrická liečebňa Samuela Bluma Plešivec. Pl-plesivec.sk. http://www.pl-plesivec.sk/hist_en.html. Accessed August 18, 2019.

58. Bideleux R, Jeffries I. *A History of Eastern Europe: Crisis and Change.* London: Routledge; 2007:473-474.

59. Beit Hatfutsot Databases. KOSICE, SLOVAKIA. Museum of the Jewish People - Beit Hatfutsot. https://dbs.bh.org.il/place/kosice-slovakia. Published 2019. Accessed August 16, 2019.

60. Williams K. *The Prague Spring and Its Aftermath: Czechoslovak Politics, 1968-1970.* Cambridge: Cambridge Univ. Press; 1999:67.

61. CIA FOIA Requests. A Look Back … The Prague Spring & the Soviet Invasion of Czechoslovakia — Central Intelligence Agency. CIA.gov. https://www cia.gov/news-information/featured-story-archive/2008-featured-story archive/a-look-back-the-prague-spring-the-soviet.html. Accessed August 15, 2019.

62. Beit Hatfutsot Databases. ROZNAVA. Museum of the Jewish People - Beit Hatfutsot. https://dbs.bh.org.il/place/roznava. Published 2019. Accessed August 16, 2019.

63. Auschwitz-Birkenau State Museum. 70.auschwitz.org. Auschwitz.org. http://70.auschwitz.org/index.php?option=com_ content&view=article&id=89&lang=en. Published 2015. Accessed August 18, 2019.

64. Eisenberg RL. El Maleh Rahamim. My Jewish Learning. https://www. myjewishlearning.com/article/el-maleh-rahamim/. Published May 5, 2009. Accessed August 18, 2019.

65. Siegel-Itzkovich J. "When trauma is passed from Holocaust victims to children." The Jerusalem Post. https://www.jpost.com/HEALTH-SCIENCE/When-trauma-is-passed-from-Holocaust-victims-to-children-549271. Published April 9, 2018. Accessed August 18, 2019.

66. Beauchamp Z. Poway synagogue shooting: the rise in deadly anti-Semitism, explained. Vox. https://www.vox.com/policyand politics/2019/5/1/18524103/poway-synagogue-shooting-anti-semitism. Published May 2019. Accessed August 18, 2019.

67. Chan M. There Are Just 100,000 Holocaust Survivors Alive Today. Time. https://time.com/4392413/elie-wiesel-holocaust-survivors-remaining/. Published July 3, 2016. Accessed August 18, 2019.

68. Wilkinson J, Hughes HS. *Contemporary Europe: A History.* Cliffs, NJ: Prentice

Hall; 1991.

69. Janek I. Hungarian Attempts at the Annexation of Slovakia in 1938 (Part I). *Social Pathology and Prevention*. 2013;1(2):51-63.

70. Rozett R. *Conscripted Slaves: Hungarian Jewish Forced Laborers on the Eastern Front during the Second World War*. Jerusalem: Yad Vashem, International Institute for Holocaust Research; 2013.

71. Montgomery JF. *Hungary: The Unwilling Satellite*. Safety Harbor, FL: Simon Publications; 2001.

72. Evans RJ. *The Third Reich at War*. Penguin Press; 2010.

73. Patai R. *The Jews of Hungary: History, Culture, Psychology*. Detroit, MI: Wayne State Univ. Press; 1999.

74. Yad Vashem. Righteous Among the Nations Honored by Yad Vashem by 1 January 2019: Slovakia. Names of Righteous by Country. https://www yadvashem.org/yv/pdf-drupal/slovakia.pdf. Published January 1, 2019. Accessed August 12, 2019.

75. Antony Beevor, *Stalingrad: The Fateful Siege: 1942-1943*. New York: Viking, 1998.

76. Yad Vashem. The Righteous Among The Nations: Lackner Imrich. http:// db.yadvashem.org/righteous/family.html?language=en&itemId=4314834. Published 2019. Accessed August 12, 2019